MENTORING
IN THE
EFFECTIVE SCHOOL

Issues in School Management Series

Marketing the Secondary School by Brent Davis and Linda Ellison
School Development Planning by Brent Davis and Linda Ellison
Managing Quality in Schools by John West-Burnham
Teacher Appraisal: Survival and Beyond by Horace Bennett
Developing Your Career in Education Management by Angela Thody
Legal Issues and the Self-Managing School by Neil Adams
Inspection: A Preparation Guide for Schools by Micheal Ormston and
Marian Shaw

MENTORING
IN THE
EFFECTIVE SCHOOL

Edited by

Pauline Smith and
John West-Burnham

LONGMAN

Published by Longman Information and Reference,
Longman Group UK Ltd, 6th Floor, Westgate House, The High,
Harlow, Essex CM20 1YR, England and Associated Companies
throughout the world.

© Longman Group UK Ltd 1993

A catalogue record for this book is available from The British Library

ISBN 0-582-22918-9

Typeset by Anglia Photoset Ltd,
34A St Botolphs Church Walk, St Botolphs Street,
Colchester, Essex CO2 7EA.

Printed in Great Britain by Redwood Books

Contents

List of contributors

Ray Acton is Head of Education Management at the Crewe+ Alsager Faculty of the Manchester Metropolitan University. He has taught in schools for 10 years, been a subject tutor in teacher training for 11 years and spent 13 years in LEA Inspectorates, becoming Chief Inspector (Doncaster LEA). His major interests are appraisal, mentoring, management styles and school inspection.

Glynn Kirkham is a Senior Lecturer in Education Management at the Crewe+Alsager Faculty of the Manchester Metropolitan University and was a former primary headteacher in Greater Manchester. He has edited a distance learning pack on school development, *Development through Action* (1990); learning material for Articled Teachers, *Working with Adults in Schools* (1992); co-authored *Mentoring – A Core Skills Pack* (1992) and wrote *A Guide to Mentoring in the Primary School* (1992). He has carried out in-service work on appraisal, evaluation and mentoring and he is currently researching headteacher development for his doctorate.

Barry Mountford has extensive experience in initial teacher education as Head of Placement, Research and Development in the Education Department of the Crewe+Alsager Faculty of the Manchester Metropolitan University. He has played a major part in developing school-Faculty partnerships through fee-contract arrangements, mentor training, competence-based approaches and profiling to link ITE to the induction of NQTs.

Pauline Smith is a Senior Lecturer in Education Management at the Crewe+Alsager Faculty of the Manchester Metropolitan University and was previously general adviser in Manchester LEA. Her interest in profiling began through work with Staffordshire TVEI and continued into Staffordshire advisory service. Present research interests include the role of appraisal, mentoring and competency-based profiling in teacher development. She is a Registered Inspector with OFSTED and is the author of *A Guide to Mentoring in the Secondary School: A Competency Based Approach* (1992) and has co-authored *Mentoring: A Core Skills Pack* (1992) and *Sociology: A Modular Approach* (1990).

Malcolm Wall has spent 13 years in schools and for the past 7 years has been general adviser with Tameside LEA. He has pastoral responsibilities for a group of schools and also for INSET and NQTs in the authority. His experience in the Articled Teachers Scheme has facilitated a close partnership with HE and development work in competency based profiling for NQTs.

John West-Burnham is Lecturer in Educational Management and Director of Distance Learning Programmes in the Education Management Development Unit of the University of Leicester. He taught in schools and colleges for 15 years, was a Principal Lecturer in Education Management in a College of Higher Education and an LEA Officer responsible for Appraisal and Management Development. He is the author of *Managing Quality in Schools* and *The Appraisal Training Resource*.

Joss West-Burnham is Senior Lecturer and Subject Pattern Leader in Cultural Studies at Crewe+Alsager Faculty of the Manchester Metropolitan University. As well as various publications in literary and cultural studies she was one of the writing team for *Through the Glass Ceiling: Effective Management Development for Women*, ed. C King, and is Co-ordinator of the Gender and the Body research network at Crewe+Alsager Faculty.

Preface

Mentoring in schools is increasingly significant because it has been identified as a major component in school-based ITE; the induction of NQTs; and its potential in appraisal, career and management development is increasingly being recognized.

The value of mentoring for professional development has long been acknowledged by industry as playing a significant role in effective professional development.

This book is a collection of essays which draw on the practical experiences and theoretical insights of mentoring and competency-based profiling from a range of individual perspectives. Each essay discusses the application of mentoring principles from differing viewpoints and raises issues for both the individual and organization in terms of the effective management of mentoring in school.

Mentoring in the Effective School contains a range of practical guidelines, suggestions for training and development and indications of how school policies and practices may be developed.

The Editors would like to thank the contributors for completing their chapters within a tight deadline and express sincere thanks to Adrienne Johnson for managing a complex manuscript.

Each contributor wishes to state that the interpretations in this book are their own.

Acknowledgements

We would like to acknowledge Cheshire LEA, particularly GEST 27 team: Marion Cheetham, Margaret Coyle, Chris Middleditch, Sylvia Selzer, with John West-Burnham; Alice Wakefield, Carol Valleley; Tameside NQT's and Mentors; and Katrina Stevens, Personnel Division, British Airways.

1 An overview and introduction to the book

Pauline Smith

Introduction

In this chapter, the author provides an overview of mentoring developments in the educational world. The argument that the establishment of an effective mentoring system in school represents a real *investment in people* is made and the links between mentoring, the Investors in People award and OFSTED inspection are explored. The chapter examines the roles, tasks and responsibilities of mentoring in schools, drawing out the implications for the selection and training of mentors and arguing that effective *communication* of these aspects lies at the heart of effective mentoring.

This section ends with the reader being invited to assess their own potential as a mentor against a range of competences of mentoring. The following section argues that *collaborative* mentoring is developmental for both the individual and the whole organisation, encouraging a climate of support, teamwork and openness that can improve morale and reduce stress levels in the teaching profession.

Finally, the author examines the role of competency-based profiling and recording of achievement practices in promoting *coherence* of development across the three key stages of a teacher's professional life — initial teacher trainee, newly qualified teacher and into continuing professional development. The value of NVQ related portfolio — building practices is considered, particularly the work of School Management South, in relation to management competences. The chapter ends with a brief examination of the role of the mentor in preparation for headship through Education Assessment Centres.

The following chapters of the book are then introduced to the reader through a summary of their main arguments and contributions to *Mentoring in the Effective School*.

Mentoring — an investment in people

From Homer's *Odyssey* onwards, there has been a generally accepted understanding that the role of mentor is to act as 'wise counsellor', 'guide', 'adviser' to younger or newer colleagues — thus, investing in their future effectiveness.

It may be true that the concept of mentoring is prone to interpretation and variation in its application (see Merriam 1983 and Jacobi 1991) which can present some difficulties for quantitative researchers. However, it is also true that mentoring has been given an important clarification by the DFE (see circulars 9/92 and administrative memorandum 2/92), in relation to its vital role in the professional development of initial trainee and newly-qualified teachers.

Yet, it is not simply the initial teacher trainees (ITTs) or, the newly qualified teachers (NQTs) that would benefit from having a mentor in school. There are clearly other groups of teachers such as the 'returners to teaching' who as the School Teachers' Review Body noted, on the advice of HMI, are a group which will increasingly need to be offered refresher courses, and support as a recent re-entrant and that 'in future individual schools will need to develop their own strategies for these activities, including access to appropriate training' (STRB 1993). An effective system of mentoring could play a vital role in providing such support and training.

Any newly-appointed member of staff in school and those moving into promoted posts, such as heads of department, bursars, deputy headteachers and headteachers are a few of the groups who face the same need for a 'wise counsellor' on the job. In fact, it can be argued that all teaching and non-teaching staff would benefit from an effective system of mentoring which provides work-related guidance and support; therefore, mentoring should be seen as a whole-school management concept.

This book considers many of the sensitive management issues surrounding mentoring in the effective school including: the partnership with HE, the selection and training issues, the use of competency-based profiling and the links between mentoring and appraisal. One of the major threads running through the book is the potential power of mentoring to bring synergy to individual and organizational management development; and the coherence in personal and professional development that can accrue through the adoption of an effective mentoring system which clearly invests in the professional development of its people.

The Employment Department clearly supports the view that the individual and the organization must develop together. Their 'Investors in People' initiative recognizes the importance of people in this development and gives support to the role of the mentor in the induction and ongoing profession development of employees in the organization:

> An Investor in People takes action to train and develop individuals on recruitment and throughout their employment. (National Standards for Effective Investment in People, ED 1993)

The philosophy underpinning this employment department initiative may well be primarily to meet the skills needs of the economy, but there are clearly additional messages for the education service to pick up on here. Education and training is not simply a matter of 'economic competitiveness', and achieving National Targets but even more critically is also a 'matter of individual fulfilment' and many teachers in schools, colleges and universities would echo Gillian Shephard's words that:

> Young people have the right to excellent standards of education and training in order to achieve to their capabilities. And those of us already in the workforce deserve relevant and structured training and development, so that we have greater choices and wider opportunities. (G. Shephard, TES 1993)

The role of guidance and advice through effective mentoring can help all employees (headteachers and teachers included) to review and identify their strengths and areas for further development; to develop skills and understanding and so to plan and implement their professional and career development (see chapter 5 for a further discussion).

At the time of writing, schools and colleges are becoming increasingly interested in registering for the 'Investors in People' award, aided perhaps by the TEC funding that is available to support this project. Its National Standards stress the importance of the School Development Plan in 'communicating to all employees a vision of where the organization is going and the contribution employees will make to its success'; and the role of appraisal in identifying job-related development needs. It can be argued that the establishment of an effective competency-based mentoring system for ITTs, NQTs and continuing professional development will help schools to achieve their Employment Department/TEC Investors in People award more speedily and that such a system may help to ensure the mutuality and synergy of individual and business goals and targets.

The need for schools to invest in the professional development of its staff and to provide support to new or inexperienced staff through, it can be argued, an effective mentoring system is also clear in the **OFSTED** evaluation criteria within the *Framework for Inspection* (DFE 1992, updated 1993).

In relation to the 'Management of Teaching Staff' inspectors will evaluate 'the extent to which there are adequate arrangements for the recruitment, retention, motivation and reward of staff members' (OFSTED Handbook 1992). The inspection team will need to consider how effective are the arrangements for staff development in meeting the needs of individual members of staff and of the school as a whole. Judgements will be made on:

> how well the school supports inexperienced staff, how thoroughly all staff understand the implications of their job descriptions and are motivated by the responsibilities delegated to them. (OFSTED Handbook Part 4 (1992)

The need for schools to formalize their induction programmes for NQTs as part of a comprehensive staff development policy and practice is clearly indicated in the OFSTED criteria. Providing a system of mentoring for NQTs; and ensuring that the job descriptions for mentors accurately reflect this important role and responsibility will go some way towards demonstrating evidence that the school values and invests in the professional development of its staff.

The necessity of clarifying the relationship between staff development and 'a well thought-out and clearly described appraisal scheme' (OFSTED 1992) is also of paramount importance in schools, especially in the light of recent Performance Related Pay developments. This book considers this important relationship in chapter 6.

It is clear to this author that an effective mentoring system can play a vital role in clarifying and ensuring a continuing investment in the professional development of teachers across the three key stages of career development — ITT, NQT and continuing professional development; and, provide evidence of such investment for an OFSTED inspection.

Before leaving these two external sources of impetus for mentoring in schools it is interesting to record that at least one school has brought the two initiatives of IIP and OFSTED together and has identified the documentary evidence that is common to both forms of external assessment. In so doing the importance of a clear induction programme; clear roles and responsibilities; appraisal and mentoring are included amongst many other training and staff development documents required for both the IIP award and the OFSTED inspection (see Table 1.1 J. A. Ashton, Standish Community High School 1993).

Table 1.1   What evidence does a school produce?

	Evidence for IIP Status	Evidence for Inspection
Letter of intent	•	
Mission Statement	•	•
Aims of School	•	•
Equal Opportunities Policy	•	•
Training Policy	•	•
Business Plan	•	•
Newsletter — IIP	•	
Employee Survey	•	
Communications Policy	•	•
Curriculum Development Plan	•	•
Training Needs Analysis	•	•
Staff Handbooks	•	•
Financial Breakdown	•	•
MCI Mentoring	•	•
Examples of Specific Training, e.g. Welfare Appraisal	•	•
Roles and Responsibilities	•	•
Induction Programme	•	•
Evidence of Staff Working in Teams	•	•
Weekly Bulletin	•	•
Health & Safety Policy and Training Record	•	•
Evidence of Evaluations	•	•
School Prospectus	•	•
Programme of Meetings	•	•
Public Exam. Results	•	•
Governors Reports	•	•
Minutes of Meetings	•	•
Training Record	•	•

© J. A. Ashton, Standish Community High School

Conclusion

In conclusion, it can be argued that leadership has a vital role to play in this 'investment in people' through the establishment of an effective mentoring system in school. A whole-school approach to mentoring, can help to promote 'a good team spirit' and to ensure that:

> new colleagues are made to feel welcome; staff are encouraged to work cooperatively with colleagues; effective support structures are in place; and those experiencing difficulties are supported. (DFE 1993)

Mentoring — communication, collaboration and coherence

Communicating the who, what and how of mentoring

Effective communication lies at the heart of effective mentoring. The need to communicate clearly to staff the tasks, roles and responsibilities of the mentor has occupied much of the training and development work engaged in by the author and other colleagues during this year. This development work was supported by GEST 27/92 Activity funding wherein this University Faculty was the named HEI in five local LEA bids and through a small DFE project grant, described in chapter 4. A whole-school approach to the management of mentoring the ITT and NQT alone, reinforces the need for the clarification and communication of the key roles and specific tasks of the mentor.

• *Who is involved?*

There are at least five possible types of mentor who could be involved in school-based mentoring:

The Subject Mentor or Classroom Mentor   This is the teacher in the school who has direct day to day responsibility for trainee or NQT in the classroom. It is often the subject head of department in secondary school or college but it could also be a designated member of that department with the appropriate skills. In primary schools, it will usually be the teacher of the class in which they are placed. The mentee would also be able to gain considerable support and guidance from the individual members of staff in the department(s) in which they are working. The subject/classteacher mentor will be involved in the observation and assessment of the trainee and newly qualified teacher.

The Professional Mentor This is usually the senior member of staff who has a responsibility for the organization of training and staff development in school. It is often the deputy head with responsibility for Professional Development Co-ordination (PDC), but whether this is appropriate has been questioned by several NQTs and deputy heads (see chapter 4). The Professional Mentor is more involved in the wider professional development of the ITT, NQT and other experienced staff, than the day-to-day training tasks carried out by subject and pastoral mentors. The Professional Mentor will, therefore, coordinate the overall training programme of mentors and mentees and will be involved in the interim summative assessments of the ITTs in relation to the 'competences of teaching' (see chapter 2).

The Pastoral Mentor This is usually the year tutor or head of house depending on the pastoral system adopted in the secondary school. The trainee and newly-qualified teacher should also have the support and guidance of the form tutor with whom they would work collaboratively, for example in the design and delivery of a PSHE programme; in relation to pupils' spiritual and moral development; in the collective act of worship and in administration and record keeping. The Pastoral Tutor could also be involved in observation and assessment of the ITT and NQT.

The HE Mentor The HE tutor has an active involvement in the mentoring process in school and needs to work closely with the Subject, Pastoral and Professional Mentors in the observation — reflection — assessment processes of the school-based ITT programme. This will require detailed planning and close collaboration based on effective working relationships. Traditionally, HE tutors have not been able to continue their involvement with trainee teachers once they have achieved QTS and have become NQTs. Now, however, the moves to a closer partnership between HEI and school will facilitate a greater continuity of mentoring support and accreditation for professional development across the ITE stage, into the induction period and beyond. Gest 17/93 partnership activity and the role of HE tutors in management consultancy work can help to provide a coherence of support and development to schools in a period of rapid change.

The LEA Mentor The LEA Adviser/Induction Coordinator can still be seen as an important mentor for the NQT. The LEA officer is able to organize and deliver a cost-effective programme of support for the NQT; although much depends on the prioritization by the school of their limited delegated funds and reinforces the need for leadership to ensure an entitlement of professional development for all its staff. Some LEA officers have gained valuable experience of providing overall mentor support to schools during the Articled Teacher Schemes which can be used effectively during the present move to school-based training.

Mentee(s)	Mentor(s)
• ITT (student-teacher)	• Subject
• NQT (Newly qualified teacher)	• Pastoral
	• Professional
	• HE
	• LEA

Figure 1.1   The mentoring role — who is involved?

In addition to the mentoring roles identified above, it has been argued earlier that mentoring, as an integral part of continuous professional development, must be seen as a whole-school activity. This view of staff development was clarified in the James Report in 1972 where it was urged that:

> every school should regard the continuous training of its teachers as an essential part of its task for which all members of staff share responsibility. (DES 1972)

The role of the mentor-colleague in facilitating this continuous professional development requires further investment this decade. Certainly, the James perspective would appear to support the notion of a 'mentoring school', where staff development is seen as central to the institutions objectives and organizational development. In such a school, all staff are likely to be involved in mentoring; the older pupils involved in mentoring the younger ones; undergraduate students come into school to mentor pupils and the value of Compact — related schemes where industry and business act as mentors to pupils in their partnership schemes will be fully recognized. (See for example the work of Salford Compact who have organized two national conferences on the use of mentoring programmes in schools, in association with the Employment Department and Whitbread plc).

• *What? — the tasks and responsibilities of mentoring*

The key tasks and responsibilities of ITT mentors must emanate from the Aim of Initial Teacher Training which is that:

> All newly qualified teachers entering maintained schools should have achieved the levels of knowledge and standards of professional competence necessary to maintain and improve standards in schools. (DFE Circular 9/92 para. 1.1 Annex A)

In other words, the ITT subject and professional mentors have joint responsibility with the HEI to ensure the progressive development of the competences of teaching through the design and delivery of appropriate learning programmes and the regular monitoring of achievement in the competences during initial training. (See chapter 2).

DFE Circular 9/92 identifies these basic competences of teaching for secondary teaching covering subject knowledge, application, class management, assessing, recording and reporting and further professionaldevelopment. HEIs, such as the Crewe+Alsager Faculty of the Manchester Metropolitan University have interpreted these competences through the integration of more detailed indicators which can then be used as an agenda for discussion between mentor and student (see Appendix 1). Annex A to the Draft Circular for the Initial Training of Primary School Teachers : New Criteria for Course Approval, dated 9 June 1993 has now identified the competences expected of primary NQTs (see Appendix 2).

These competences have been enhanced by this University through the addition of the competency of 'Critical Self-Reflection' which surprisingly was absent from the DFE list. The importance of the 'reflexive practitioner' cannot surely be overstated and is fully supported through the work of Duignan 1987, Schon 1987, and many other researchers. Further development work between school and HE mentors is now concentrating on sharing an interpretation of the competences and agreeing what constitutes acceptable evidence of achievement.

These DFE Competences of Teaching have also been used as a basis for the NQT profiles developed throughout this year using GEST 27 funding activity. Chapter 3 provides a detailed case-study of this development work in Tameside LEA which evidences the potential coherence in professional development promoted through competency-based profiling under-pinning mentoring.

The use of the Professional Development Profile as a major source of evidence of achievement and as a vehicle for the development of the skills of critical self-reflection, joint review and target-setting is promoted for both ITTs and NQTs through DFE advice;

and is also evident in the portfolio-building associated with NVQ related management competency schemes, such as Management Charter Initiative and School Management South, which are discussed later in this chapter. Undoubtedly, the skills of the mentor in using the profile in joint review and target-setting sessions are vital to the professional development of the mentee.

• How? — the skills of mentoring

If the main tasks of mentoring are to help the ITT/NQT develop the necessary knowledge, understanding, skills and relationships involved in competent teaching, then mentors need also to be 'trainers' as well as 'guides' and 'wise counsellors'.

The success of school-based training and staff development can be highly dependent on the knowledge, skills and personal qualities of the professional and subject/class mentors. Therefore, once roles are clarified there is a need to concentrate on the *selection and training* of the mentor. This investment in the professional development of the mentor is likely to reveal the importance of *how adults learn*, including *needs identification* and *action research skills*; the value of *positive relationships* and the importance of communication skills to ensure that *constructive feedback* and appropriate *target setting* takes place.

The role of *negotiation* in establishing a clear focus for further professional development has formed a key part of the training courses for mentors provided by the author this year. The generic value of this skills training in relation to appraisal and management development is further explored in Chapters 5 and 6. Similarly, the role of the *Professional Development Profile* in developing the skills of the reflexive practitioner has proved vitally important. Critical *self assessment* lies at the heart of the teacher development process and the mentor must have the skills and understanding to promote and develop this practice through demonstrating its use.

Furthermore, the need to raise mentee *self esteem* and to encourage the identification of strengths is vital and requires a careful pairing of mentor/mentee with considerations of gender, personality, experience and position being taken into account. A careful selection and training of the mentor in relation to these qualities, in order to fulfil the potential of equal opportunity of development for all teachers, is clearly highlighted and explored further in chapter 4.

The value of constructive feedback in the *formative assessment* provided by the mentor for ITT and NQT cannot be over-emphasized. Yet, the potential *conflict* that is perhaps inherent in the role of mentor where both formative and summative assessment responsibilities exist still needs to be fully researched; and supports the need for an early clarification and agreement of roles and tasks between all partners in the mentoring process.

As an aside, it is interesting to note that the 'buddies' who play an essential role in the staff development programme of British Airways appear not to suffer role conflict in their mentoring role. They provide a weekly report on their programme participants in terms of their standard of performance, assessed according to three levels of achievement: 'a strength', 'acceptable' or 'an area for improvement'; yet, the Buddy's Contract is:

- To act as a role model
- To be responsible for 'hands on' training
- To be committed to helping the individual in the development
- To give honest feedback
- To frequently liaise with the client representative

The similarities between these roles and responsibilities and those of the school based mentor seem apparent — at least in the first four! Although, comparisons between the on-the-job training of one service industry with another are practically impossible, nevertheless perhaps something is to be gained from an appreciation of the fact that a BA 'Buddy's Report' is just one element in their staff development programme which includes: self-teaching and assessment; computer-based training; shadowing; coaching and behavioural skills training (The Programme, K Stevens 1993). British Airways would appear to be investing in its people through the use of a wide range of training and development techniques. Will our school-based mentors be adequately resourced to allow the same investment in the professional development of teachers?

The establishment of a whole school staff development policy which supports the practice of a wide-range of professional development activities is likely therefore to see the role of mentor as central to the process and one that can ensure a coherence in the review and evaluation of such activities.

Schools with this effective holistic approach are likely to recognize the importance of mentorship in their school development plan and will take seriously the selection and training of its mentors.

Conclusion

This section has attempted to communicate some of the vital tasks, roles, responsibilities and skills of mentoring and has stressed the importance of a whole-school approach to mentorship. As a final activity, the questionnaire (see Figure 1.2) uses many of the

Figure 1.2   The competences of mentoring

Assessing Mentoring Potential — assess your own potential as a mentor or the mentoring potential of colleagues. Indicate on the continuum whether this is a strength or an area for further development.

1) **A good role model**
   Someone to be respected through ability/experience/willingness to self-review

   (an area for further development)   a strength

2) **An enthusiast**
   Someone who sparks interest; makes teaching fascinating

   (an area for further development)   a strength

3) **An identifier of need**
   Helps the mentee to identify areas of further development; to prioritise needs and set appropriate targets

   (an area for further development)   a strength

4) **A teacher-guide**
   Show mentee how to improve; share skills, discusses issues, ideas and problems willingly

   (an area for further development)   a strength

Figure 1.2 *Continued*

5) **A problem-solver**
Helps mentee to identify their strengths and shows how to use them to overcome problems and further improve

(an area for further development)   a strength

6) **A supporter**
A good listener; warm and caring; encouraging and accessible; a counsellor

(an area for further development)   a strength

7) **A manager of conflict**
A good negotiator; aware of the politics of the institution

(an area for further development)   a strength

8) **A career counsellor**
Good at helping the mentee to sort out their career pathway

(an area for further development)   a strength

competences (knowledge, skills, attitudes and values) identified as being important in facilitating mentee development. Use the questionnaire to assess your own potential as a mentor, or to assess the mentoring potential of colleagues.

The challenge for collaboration

The three way partnership of schools, HE and LEA in NQT mentoring during the past year has inevitably brought its own challenges of effective communication and collaboration. Similarly, there are complex contractual arrangements for ITT school-based training involving selecting the schools; clarifying the programmes and identifying and training the subject, professional and HE mentors.

Collaboration in NQT development work has become yet more challenging during 1993/4 through increased delegation of GEST funds so that schools can only be 'invited' and 'influenced' to regard NQT development as a priority for investment — rather than directed more strongly by LEAs.

The potential (or real) competition between HEI and LEA as providers of mentor training is another possible barrier to collaboration. This competition has been kept somewhat at bay in Manchester Metropolitan University and its partner LEAs through the DFE Project work which has involved five local authorities (see chapter 3) and through the positive working relationships that have allowed a beneficial sharing of expertise and experience. For example, a recent conference in Manchester allowed a sharing of developments across the faculties of this university (some 35 miles apart at the time of writing) and inputs from three of the eight LEAs with which it is working on competency-based profiles and induction. Joint HE/ LEA mentor training has taken place in all but one of the eight partner LEAs.

However, money may yet prove to be divisive to these beneficial collaborations. Although GEST 17 holds out a straw of hope for the continuation of these recent partnerships in NQT developments, other government 'initiatives' relating to on-the job teacher training, for example the proposals in relation to one year courses for nursery and Key Stage 1 QTS, appear to be damaging to the barely established system of school-based training embodied in circular 9/92 (DFE, Secondary PGCE) and to any real partnership with HEI's (see chapter 2 for a further discussion).

However, if 'partnership' may have become devalued through political changes in teacher education, the need for the profession to recognize the importance of 'mutuality of purpose' in the professional development of its teachers clearly has not.

A continuity of support across the three key stages of teacher development, is encouraged through DFE Circulars and GEST activities. Through the partnership work described in this book it is possible to witness the early development of a potentially more coherent, continuous and accumulative system of support and accreditation for teacher professional development than has existed to date. Collaboration between HE, LEA and schools clearly has the potential to provide mutual benefits to the profession as a whole.

Furthermore, the clustering of schools through the PGCE model and beyond can encourage collaboration across the schools allowing ITTs, NQTs and their school/HE mentors the opportunity to meet and share experiences; and to organize cluster in-service training.

There are also some early signs that HEIs and LEAs will continue to collaborate through their GEST 17 activity funding during 1993/94. For example, locally, there is a willingness and a need to collaborate on the evaluation and further development of the competency-based profiles and mentor training used by their joint schools. Whilst nationally, Margaret Wilkin's initiative of setting up regionally based 'Area Groups for ITT' (AGIT) has, at the time of writing, real promise for voluntary and meaningful collaboration between consortia of HE institutions, schools and other interested groups such as industry and TECs. (M. Wilkin, Cambridge UDE 1993). Richard Pomeroy at Wolverhampton University has already produced an analysis of the national survey of current and anticipated mentor training programmes in HEIs and is willing to act as a link for the establishment of regional consortia in school-based ITT, thus aiding collaboration and a sharing of expertise.

The benefits to the profession of an open and collaborative culture are of course well documented — see for example the recent DFE summary of the NDC/CREATE Project funded on advice from the former School Management Task Force and supported by the Associations in the Professional Working Party which reveals that the criteria for an effectively managed school includes:

> . . . a concern to build a learning environment for staff as well as students. Teachers strive to improve on their professional practice; they regularly discuss teaching methods in detail, engage in joint planning, prepare learning materials together, are encouraged to share ideas, experiences and successes, and both seek and give advice. (DFE 1993)

Such collaboration in teaching and learning lies at the heart of effective mentoring and is, it can be argued, the life blood of the effectively-managed school.

An open collaborative culture and a supportive climate is vital in schools which are 'people processing' rather than 'product processing' organizations (Katz and Kahn 1978); and many researchers have identified the importance of *team work* as part of this 'culture of collaboration' (see the work of Nias, Southwork and Yeomans 1989 and Weindling and Earley 1987 amongst many others).

A team can be said to have two main characteristics in that it has a common shared purpose: a job to perform; and that it requires team members to work together in a relationship of trust and interdependence. The professional, pastoral and subject mentors within a large secondary school, for example, must work together as a team of mentors since no one mentor will have the skills and knowledge that is required for this comprehensive training. Similarly, the mentoring relationship of mentor–mentee can be likened to the 'team' in spirit if not in size! There is clearly a shared purpose in the development of the mentee; and clearly, interdependence and effective working relationships are required for the successful achievement of these goals.

Effective mentoring relationships, it can be argued, are built on the quality of the inter-personal and communication skills, demonstrated particularly by the *mentor as leader*, wherein an open climate with real opportunity for listening, problem-solving and consideration of the views and reflections of the mentee is encouraged; that is, the 'reflective practitioner' skills identified by Schon 1987. Such 'educative' leadership which can exist at all positions in the school is most likely to motivate the mentee and to 'build the team' through an open willingness to share information, experience and expertise; thus: 'identifying what is worth doing and preferred ways of doing and acting in education' (Duignan and Macpherson 1987).

The constructive advice given by a group of teachers to headteachers in general and recorded by Guy Claxton in 1989 is supportive of this need for a climate of collaboration and openness in schools when they said:

> . . . when you have good grounds for thinking that something isn't right, tell us. We may not like it, but we would rather know. We won't be straight with you if you aren't straight with us . . . conversely, let us know when you like what we've done . . . 'we suspect that part of your humanness is that you would like the odd bit of recognition or the occasional compliment too. Can you let us do it, or do you have to be strong and silent? . . . (Claxton 1989)

The importance of constructive feedback for all teachers, whether new experienced or senior managers, is clearly highlighted through these teachers' words. Constructive feedback is one of the skills identified earlier in this chapter as being vitally important in developing an open, mentoring climate in school.

A school leadership that encourages this sort of openness and listens to the advice (and compliments!) of its teachers is also most likely to support the views expressed by J Dunham (1992) and other writers, in relation to *stress management*, where they argue for the 'deliberate development of the social climate and social support within schools'. Kyriacou (1987) citing the work of other researchers in the field of 'teacher stress' emphasizes that the most frequently advocated management strategies for reducing teacher stress in school includes:

— Better organization and communication within the school
— An improved climate of support
— More effective programmes of staff induction and professional development
— More recognition of teacher efforts and a clearer description of job tasks and expectations

It is clear, therefore, that there are real benefits in terms of stress management for both the individual and the organization in adopting an open and collaborative approach to human resource management and ongoing professional development — which can clearly be aided by the adoption of an effective mentoring programme of support.

The benefits of mentoring for the teaching profession can perhaps be illuminated by the recent work on 'mentorship/ preceptorship' in the nursing profession. Two of the author's in-service students are nurse tutors and have trained and written in this field of preceptorship introduced recently by the UK Central Council for Nursing, Midwifery and Health Visiting; the author is indebted to these students for the following insights into this related field of mentoring.

The Central Council's policy document identifies the need for all newly qualified staff to be provided with:

a period of support for approximately the first four months of practice . . . under the guidance of a preceptor. (Annex One to registrar's letter 1/1993)

The preceptor is 'a first level nurse, midwife or health visitor who has at least twelve months or equivalent experience within the same or associated clinical field.' The policy goes on to state that:

The preceptor should be seen as a guide and supporter for the newly registered practitioner; a colleague who can act as a valuable source of help, both professionally and personally during the early and uncertain months of registered practice. (Ibid)

It is interesting to note that the Council recognizes that preceptors will require specific preparation for their role and also that many experienced nurses, midwives and health visitors will already have acquired some of these skills and recommends therefore not more than two days training to prepare for the role of preceptor. Similarities, perhaps, across the professions in terms of government funding for mentor training!

At a recent training programme for preceptorship held by M Cameron, the benefits of mentoring for the mentor, mentee and the nursing service were identified by participants. These benefits make interesting comparisons with those identified by NQTs and professional mentors in schools at a recent training event delivered by the author.

Nursing profession

Mentee   The benefits of having a mentor include:
— *You have a ready-made relationship*
— *It is beneficial to learning (having some-one who is interested in you)*
— *You feel secure (knowing some-one will protect you from making mistakes)*
— *You have some-one with local knowledge of staff and patients*
— *They can help you develop insight*
— *They give you open feedback on your progress*
— *They give you encouragement*
— *It avoids a lot of stress having a mentor*
— *It fosters collaborative practice*
— *Someone to advocate for you*

Mentor   The benefits of having a mentee include:
— *Increased job satisfaction*
— *It encourages you to keep your feet on the ground*
— *Helps you develop personnel management skills (sensitivity to the needs of others)*
— *Promotes reflection and self development*
— *Encouragement to keep up to date*
— *Teaching skills can be further developed*
— *Interchange of experiences*
— *Promotes responsibility*
— *Promotes pride in your nursing skills*
— *Career development*

Nursing Profession   The benefits of mentoring include:
— *Better quality service (more thoughts behind action)*
— *Better relationships between staff*
— *Opportunities for staff development*
— *More scrutinisation of policies/procedures*
— *It boosts morale and promotes rivalry between areas*
— *It is cost effective*

(M Cameron 1993)

Teaching profession

Mentee   The benefits of mentoring include:
— *Having a medium through which to address ideas to senior management*
— *Providing support, consolation, sympathy, constructive feedback*
— *The opportunity to share achievements and failures*
— *Time to observe other teachers at work*
— *Opportunity to be reflective on performance*
— *Non-threatening guidance*
— *Feeling less isolated within an established staff*
— *Meeting other NQTs*
— *Having someone to talk to*

Mentor   The benefits of mentoring include:
— *Makes you evaluate the quality of your teaching/planning*
— *Develops appraisal skills*
— *Keeping in touch with the problems of NQTs*
— *An opportunity to be reflective on own performance*
— *Good experience for career development*
— *Increased status and responsibilities*
— *Increasing your enthusiasm*
— *Providing new ideas*

Teaching Profession   The benefits of mentoring include:
— *Well adjusted teachers*
— *Good networks*
— *Improved relationships between staff/team-building*
— *Identification of communication/organization problems in the school*
— *Likely to entice more people into profession and improve its status*

(P Smith and M Wall 1993)

The benefits of collaborative mentoring practice during a challenging and potentially stressful period of transition can clearly be identified in the benefits identified for the newly-qualified member of staff — whether nurse or teacher. Similarly, the opportunity for reflection and self development afforded through the open sharing of experiences is clearly valued by mentors within both teaching and nursing services.

Conclusion

In conclusion, as the School Management Task Force stated in 1990, the most important asset of any organization must be the people who work in it and to 'develop those people is to increase that asset'.

Collaborative mentoring, it has been argued, is developmental for both the individual and the whole organization encouraging a climate of support, team work and openness which may well lead to improvements in teacher morale, stress levels and address some of the serious retention issues facing the profession in certain geographical and subject areas (School Teacher Review Body 1993). This section argues that collaboration across the partners in mentoring-schools, HEIs and LEAs, is not only possible but essential in providing a continuity of support for professional development during a period of turbulence and change.

The potential for coherence

The development of profiling and recording of achievement practices across the three key stages of a teacher's professional life ITT, NQT and CPD (Continuing Professional Development) must represent one of the major thrusts for coherence and continuity of teacher development this century.

The ITT stage of development

Student teachers have been entering HEIs in recent years fully conversant in Records of Achievement (RoA) through their own school experiences. Within the next twelve months, students will be entering HE with their National Records of Achievement (NRAs) and will be expecting their university and school to help them to continue this life-long process of profiling achievements and setting targets for further development. (Manchester Metropolitan University is, in fact, now involved in a pilot project to accredit the RoA processes of 11–16 and 16–18 neighbouring institutions which it hopes to extend over the next twelve months.

Over the past three to four years, many HEIs have introduced Professional Development Profiles into their ITT courses (see chapter 2). A range of competences have been developed by course teams, based on CATE/DFE advice and clarified by Circular 9/92 for secondary and the Draft Circular for primary competences and teaching. Students have been encouraged to self-reflect, joint-review and target-set their further development; observation schedules have been constructed and the school experience tutor and teacher encouraged to provide constructive feedback to the student on the basis of these clear competences of teaching.

The NQT stage of development

The progression of competency-based profiles into the NQT stage of development has been greatly facilitated by the GEST 27/92 and 17/93 funding arrangements. LEA working groups, seconded through GEST and working in close partnership with HEI staff have used these Competences of Teaching as the basis for the further development of an NQT profile of competences (see chapter 4 for a case study of this development).

This profile of teaching competences is, of course. just one element in the Professional Development Portfolios (PDP) developed by LEA staff in conjunction with HEI tutors. Other sections of the portfolios include suggestions for school-based NQT induction programmes ; and all identify the key role played by the mentor in the coherent and continuous professional development of the new teacher.

Cheshire LEA's PDP entitled *The First Year of Teaching* is a good example of the support and guidance provided for schools in their NQT mentoring role. Section 5 of this portfolio is entitled *Mentoring in Primary and Secondary Schools* and its contents are replicated below.

Mentoring in Primary and Secondary Schools —
Cheshire LEA
Contents

(1) A Definition of Mentoring

(2) Effective Mentoring through an understanding of:
    (i)   The Whole-School Management of the Process of mentoring
    (ii) The Selection of the Mentor

    (iii)   The Role of the Mentor
    (iv)   Working Towards an Understanding of the Competences of Teaching
     (v)   Strategies for Managing a Competence-Based Approach

(3) The Training Needs of the Mentor:
     (i)   Identification of the Necessary Skills
    (ii)   Developing the Generic Skills of:
- Observing
- Listening
- Providing Constructive Feedback
- Negotiating
- Problem-Solving
- Managing Stress
- Target Setting

    (iii)   Meeting the Challenges of Mentoring

(4) A Checklist for Mentors

Cheshire's section on 'The Role of the Mentor' is worthy of recording here since it clearly reinforces the key responsibility of the mentor for the continuous professional development of the NQT through the effective use of profiling skills, particularly self review.

Cheshire LEA — The Role of the Mentor

> After taking up appointment the NQT should be able, so far as is practicable, to seek help and guidance from a nominated member of staff who has been adequately prepared for the role . . . (Administrative Memorandum 2/92 DFE)

Some of the constituents of this role are listed here, but individual schools may wish to modify these to meet their own specific school circumstances.

- To welcome the **NQTs** into the school and to help familiarise them with the procedures and practices of that school
- To provide regular opportunities for formal and informal meetings with appropriate members of staff
- To be responsible for offering professional, social and domestic support
- To encourage, motivate and create a positive and supportive climate
- To access opportunities for the **NQT** to observe examples of excellent practice both within and outside the school

- To facilitate opportunities to network with other **NQTs** in other schools
- To develop and apply effective procedures for classroom observation
- To use effectively lists of competences/abilities to provide the agenda for meaningful and focussed dialogue with the mentee
- To encourage actively the mentee to reflect and self-evaluate
- To identify specific needs and to undertake personally or make arrangements for school-based development and support activities
- To assist the mentee with updating the Professional Development Profile
- To help the New Teacher recognise and accept his/her responsibilities with regard to performance, effect and development
- To applaud and celebrate achievement
- To help other staff realise their potential for contribution to new teachers' development
- To attend relevant **INSET** activities. (Cheshire LEA 1993)

The next section in Cheshire's PDP goes on to propose strategies for managing a competency-based approach to NQT development and recognizes the importance of 'appraisal skills' in mentoring and of the mentor adopting and using a PDP themselves.

The third stage — continuing professional development

At this moment of writing, the potential for the coherent progression of profiling practice into the years beyond the NQT period remains unproven.

The progression of self-assessment, observation, review and target-setting skills are clearly possible through the appraisal. However, the prime purpose of appraisal for 'professional development' stands the risk of being compromised through the introduction of Performance Related Pay (PRP) into schools and colleges. The need to keep professional development practices separate from PRP practices may therefore mean the need for teachers to separate mentoring from appraisal. Yet, skills and the use of competency-based profiling can underpin both processes and often the same personnel will be involved! Chapter 6 goes on to argue that in order to protect the professional benefits of appraisal, evidenced to date, we need to introduce the concept of the mentor–appraiser, to re-examine the elements of the appraisal process and to enhance its formative nature by the incorporation of mentoring principles.

Profiling or portfolio building, for the experienced teacher is however clearly in evidence in the teaching profession through NVQ related developments. The Institute of Training and Development Assessor and Verifier Awards (1992), (D32, D33 in particular) are proving to provide relevant vehicles for the recording and accreditation of assessment experience for practising teachers and lecturers. In the future, it is possible that all ITT students will be encouraged to engage in this NVQ related portfolio building. The links between NVQ work-based competencesand the DFE Competences of Teaching — particularly 'Assessing, Recording and Reporting' are clearly in evidence; and, further NVQ related developments in profiling, particularly in relation to the 'management' competences, are gaining in popularity and providing a coherent vehicle of professional development support.

The school management competences developed by School Management South (SMS) as a result of a regional pilot project funded by LEAs and the ED and led by Peter Earley has provided a valuable stimulus to the competency-based profiling debate. Working from the Management Charter Initiative (MCI) Management 2 Generic Competences and using a functional analysis of school management, the SMS team identified ten Units of Competence relating to the Key Roles of managing 'policy', 'learning', 'people' and 'resources'. These units are then broken down into more specific 'elements' of competence against which managers can self reflect and gather evidence of achievement in relation to their performance, knowledge and understanding (see appendix 3).

Element C2.2 'Identify, review and improve development activities for individuals' is clearly a competence relevant to the school-based mentor and the detailed 'performance criteria' and 'range statements' provided for the candidate give clear guidance on what is successful performance (see P. 21 Standards for School Management 1992). SMS suggest that assessment of performance in the course of normal work is the most natural form of evidence of competence and the work-based profile assessment of the mentor's management competence is an interesting dimension to further pursue over future months.

The role of the mentor in competency-based profiling is clearly identified by the SMS project director, in that:

> Mentors will be expected to engage in a debate about the sources and forms of evidence encouraging learners to be inventive with the evidence submitted, as well as advising on its adequacy for assessment purposes. (P. Earley 1992)

The main sources of evidence of achievement gathered into a portfolio include: personal reflective reports, witness testimonies, products such as an induction/development programme and directly observed demonstrations. There are, of course, clear links in this process of evidence collection with elements in the ITT and appraisal processes necessitating future exploration.

The SMS Management Competency Project team provide an important source of advocacy for the vital role of mentoring in the continuing professional development of managers at all levels in the school system. The success of a competency-based approach to training and development hinges largely, they argue, on the

> quality of the relationships between mentors and learners. . . . Good mentors are characterized by such factors as their accessibility, the support they give, their knowledge of the learner and the fact that the mentoring role is seen as an integral part of their own job responsibilities. (P. Earley 1992)

The active role of mentors in negotiation, counselling and supporting candidates is stressed by SMS and it is interesting to note that a separation of the counselling and judgmental roles is encouraged; and that the counselling function of mentoring is considered to be more important than any final assessment role.

Finally, in relation to the potential for coherent and continuing professional development through competency-based profiling and mentoring, mention should be made of the headteacher mentoring schemes provided by LEAs during the last decade which have given valuable support to new headteachers.

Many LEAs have encouraged the role of mentor head and the involvement of this mentor from the advertisement stage into the first year of headteacher appointment and beyond. In the past, sources of GEST funding have allowed the mentor head to build a relationship with the mentee through the use of informal meetings, work shadowing and to provide professional support of a peer or co-counselling nature. The question of whether the school will decide to prioritize this 'need' for professional support and agree to fund this valuable mentoring practice in the future remains to be seen.

The North-West Executive Mentoring Group is an organization which grew out of the School Management Task Force. Local LEAs have used the five day mentor training programme provided by NWEMG to train their mentor heads; but, again the future funding of this service remains uncertain.

Lastly, the development of Education Assessment Centres (EAC) in Britain during the 90s can also be cited as evidence of the value of competency-based profile assessment and the role of mentoring in the coherent and progressive development of senior managers.

The EAC process provides candidates with a detailed diagnostic

profile of their current level of performance across a range of twelve
key competences for school leadership. The profile can then be used
by the participant alongside other sources of evidence such as
appraisal discussions, to plan a programme of further professional
development. (Green et al. 1991)

The EAC initiative trains experienced heads as mentors who then
provide guidance and support for the management development of a
colleague (the protegee) by 'a planned programme of on the job
experience, possibly supplemented by off-site experience, and
linked to regular meetings for analysis, reflection and further
planning' (ibid.). It is argued that this sort of continuous approach to
management development is far more effective and coherent than
the annual performance review or appraisal; and there is evidence
that some MBA courses, supported perhaps by the GM/Independent
sector, are using EACs as part of their programme of development.
(Chapter 7 discusses further the role of assessment centres and the
American experiences of this initiative.)

Whilst the future of EACs in Britain remains uncertain due to
the high costs involved in the process, nevertheless the vital role
played by mentoring in the preparation for school leadership has
been clearly identified by the Oxford Education Assessment Centre
whose booklet *Assessment and Mentoring for Headship* also stresses the
importance of leaders having a strong commitment to the value of
'life long learning' and a clear vision for the future thus ensuring a
coherent and unified strategy for management. (H. Green et al.
1991.)

Conclusion

Life-long learning and continuous professional development for all
teachers it has been argued in this section and beyond can be aided
by the sensitive use of competency-based profiling underpinned by
an effective mentoring system.

The chapters which follow provide further support for the
arguments expressed in this overview and introduction. The need
for further 'investment in people' and the potential role played by
mentoring in the professional development of new and experienced
teachers and managers is explored through several of the chapters
outlined below. Similarly, the need for clear 'communication' of
roles in the complex partnerships; for continued 'collaboration' both
inside and outside the school and for a 'coherence' of professional
development across the three key stages of a teacher-manager's
career is echoed by all the contributors.

A summary of the following chapters

Chapter 2

In this chapter, Barry Mountford argues that the teacher-mentor has a pivotal role to play in ensuring the future quality of initial teacher training as it increasingly becomes more school-based.

The history and context of school-based initial teacher education outlined and the partnership issues of HE and school are fully explored. The chapter ends with a consideration of the implications of school-based training for the role of mentor in both secondary and primary schools and identifies many of the important skills training issues to be managed over the next few years.

Chapter 3

In this chapter, Malcolm Wall and Pauline Smith demonstrate the value of a partnership approach to the mentoring of newly qualified teachers. The importance of building on a tradition of competency based profiling introduced through the articled teacher scheme is highlighted and issues in the design and delivery of both NQT and mentor training programmes are discussed. The chapter ends with an evaluation of the 'ideal induction programme' and reviews the design of the LEA professional development profile.

Chapter 4

In this chapter, Ray Acton, Pauline Smith and Glynn Kirkham provide insights into the mentor training programmes designed and delivered by HE lecturers during the academic year 1992/3. The value of the partnership with LEA, through GEST and DFE project funded work is also considered and the chapter ends with a summary of the major management issues raised through the training sessions and beyond.

Chapter 5

In this chapter, Pauline Smith and Joss West-Burnham reveal the importance of the skills of self-review, target-setting and action planning in the personal and career development of teachers. The vital role of skilled and sensitive mentors in this process of career guidance for both male and female managers in the classroom and beyond is discussed; and the argument that mentoring can help to advance equality of opportunity for women's professional development in the teaching profession is explored.

Chapter 6

In this chapter, John West-Burnham and Pauline Smith explore the relationship between teacher appraisal in schools and the mentoring process. It analyses the Appraisal Regulations and identifies an approach to them which encourages a developmental approach and argues that the introduction of mentoring techniques and relationships enhances and sophisticates the appraisal process. Without such enhancement there is a very real danger that school teacher appraisal will become a power/coercive bureaucratic model or an ineffectual chore. The incorporation of mentoring principles into appraisal practices can help create a genuinely developmental approach which has the potential to support real change and personal and professional growth.

Chapter 7

In this chapter, Glynn Kirkham justifies the need for headteachers to have mentors. Drawing on the work of Daresh and Playko (1992, 1993) in theUnited States and their consultancy work in Britain, the skills of headship and headship mentoring are explored. Developments in headteacher mentoring are presented and recommendations for future action are propounded.

Chapter 8

In this chapter, John West-Burnham explores the relationship between the concept of effective management development and the culture and techniques of mentoring. The chapter develops a definition of management development, identifies the relationship between this definition and mentoring and then proposes a number of strategies to support management development using mentoring techniques.

2 Mentoring and initial teacher education

Barry Mountford

Introduction

In this chapter, the author argues that the teacher-mentor has a pivotal role to play in ensuring the future quality of initial teacher training as it increasingly becomes more school-based.

The history and context of school-based initial teacher education are outlined and the partnership issues of HE and school are fully explored. The chapter ends with a consideration of the implications of school-based training for the role of mentor in both secondary and primary schools and identifies many of the important skills training issues to be managed over the next few years.

The background to school-based initial teacher education

School-based initial teacher education has both a history and a context.

Over the past decade or so a number of concerns and influences have been exercised on the relative merits of Higher Education Institutions (HEIs) and schools as locations for the training of teachers.

- Teachers and headteacher associations in their annual conferences seeking more involvement in ITE

- The Council for the Accreditation of Teacher Education (CATE) influence in setting out criteria for courses including length of time in schools
- HEI concerns to make training more relevant to student and school needs
- HMI surveys such as *The New Teacher in School* (1988, 1992)
- Political debate on the value of 'theory' to intending teachers; concerns translated into circulars (e.g., 24/89, 9/92) to transfer funding and training to schools

An impression is often given, sometimes gained and seldom publicly challenged, 'that HEIs are reluctant partners in these events'. Crewe+Alsager Faculty, for example, has been involved in enhancing school-based training via 'fee-contract' arrangements with schools. Our training programme anticipated the introduction of both competence-based approach and profiling by CATE by some three years.

Recent national initiatives in school-based training are set out below:

- 1991   — School-based Initial Teacher Training (ITT) in England and Wales. A report by HMI
- January 1992   — Kenneth Clark (then Secretary of State) outlined his ideas for the reform of ITT in a speech to the North of England Conference
                              — a DES consultation paper followed
- May 1992   — John Patten (Secretary of State at the time of writing) announced details of reform to Secondary courses for implementation by September 1994
- June 1992   — DFE Circular 9/92 (Welsh Office 35/92) Initial Teacher Training (Secondary Phase) was published outlining procedures and criteria for secondary ITT and procedures for primary ITT
- November 1992 — Note of guidance (relating to circular 9/92, 35/92) issued by CATE on the partnerships between HEIs and schools, accreditation criteria and institutional planning for ITT
- May 1993   — CATE consultation paper on primary ITT criteria
- September 1993 — The Government's proposals for the Reform of Initial Teacher Training (DFE)

The principle of school-based training for intending teachers has a broad spectrum of support including HMI, headteacher associations, teacher associations, training institutions, schools, students and politicians, albeit for somewhat different reasons. Commitment to a principle is one thing, effective implementation in its detail is something else. There are a number of issues relating to the partnership between schools and training institutions which are at the heart of school-based training.

Partnership issues in school-based ITE

The effectiveness of school-based training for intending teachers rests on more than just extending time in schools. As HMI put it:

> The concept of school-based training should not merely be a quantitive one but should include also the quality of teacher involvement in planning, providing and assessing training and the quality of co-operation between higher education and schools. (School-based ITT in England and Wales. DES 1991, paragraph 76)

An apprenticeship model is unsuitable for professional training. Being a teacher involves much more than being an effective class-room performer, important though this is. Professionals understand the context they are operating in and their role in the general scheme of things. Increasingly teaching is a team activity so the ability to work with adults as well as children is important. If we are to be concerned with defining school based training as more than additional teaching practice, we also need to be clear about the key issues which underpin this concern with quality of partnership provision. These issues include:

- *A recognition that the prime purpose of schools is to teach pupils not train teachers*

It follows from this that partnerships with schools need to develop with staff and governors involvement. A proper and balanced involvement in school-based ITT will be recognised in any school development plan, for example.

- *Schools need to be carefully chosen*

The conditions and present circumstances of some schools render them unsuitable for involvement in teacher training schemes. HMI report that a third of what goes on in schools is 'unsatisfactory' and on these grounds alone there is a need to screen applications from schools to become involved in training. This is not simply a matter of identifying 'unsuitable' schools but more likely it will involve identifying suitable departments within schools.

There is some doubt whether the existing arrangements for identifying partner schools is adequate in this respect. Schools interested in partnership are invited to approach HEIs. Where HEIs do not accept a school offer of partnership, they should make clear their reasons for their decision. The Secretary of State reserves the right to withhold approval from an institution's courses of ITT if there were evidence that individual schools had been treated arbitrary or unreasonably.

Involving schools in initial teacher education is a volume as well as a quality operation. At any one time there are over 40,000 students training to be teachers, many of these requiring two school placements in the year. Matching school offers of placements to student needs (subject, professional development and home-base locations) is a complex task.

Most institutions rely on information based on historical use, reports from tutors and students' advice from LEA officers. Primary schools, because of their size, can only accept one or two students at a time. Secondary schools have subject specific difficulties. Suitable placements in shortage subjects — because they are shortage subjects — are sometimes difficult to find and tend to be overwhelmed by approaches from several institutions. The constraints of a fixed budget further compromise a satisfactory placement and student experience.

All ITE courses are required to provide for experience in more than one school. This acknowledges the differences between schools and the need for students to develop a range of approaches to teaching. The location of some HEIs does provide for diversity of school experience in urban, rural and ethnic minority communities.

There is little doubt that placing students for school experience is becoming more difficult. So called 'negotiated agreements' over catchment areas are breaking down. There is widespread encroachment with many schools being approached by several institutions to accommodate students. The pressure of the National Curriculum and its assessment lead to staff absenteeism and high turnover making schools reluctant to add to the discontinuity of the children's curriculum experience. An increasing number of schools are refusing to take students under any circumstances and this may be damaging to the longer term prospects for enhanced diversity and quality in placements.

As HMI point out (DES 1991, paragraph 41):

> After quality, the issue of greatest concern in school placement is good communication.

This concern is less to do with the written guidelines which all institutions provide for schools than with the use made of this material. Frequently the teacher closest to the students' school experience has not received or read the documentation. Consequently they are at a disadvantage in offering course and student related support. Schools used for placement of students on different courses e.g., BEd and PGCE, find this problem increases. Given the substantial nature of the documents accompanying the implementation of the National Curriculum, which has a much higher priority than student experience, it is perhaps not surprising then that the school placement material is not read even if it gets passed on. Clearly the faculty-based mentor has a major responsibility to ensure that school-based mentors understand their role clearly. Increasingly the student must be encouraged to take a more active role in explaining and defining the support she/he needs, based on professional developments identified as an outcome of previous school experiences.

- *School-based mentors will need to be carefully chosen*

Not all teachers are able or willing to take on this training role. The most suitable are likely to be the most experienced and successful and will have many other demands on their time. Headteachers and governors will be concerned about the impact of the involvement of key staff on children's learning.

Such teachers need high status in the school, not only as classroom practitioners but also influential in providing whole-school support for the students.

- *Teachers need time and training for their role*

Some of the ITE mentor training relates to other development initiatives e.g., newly qualified teachers (NQT) induction and appraisal. Training in classroom observation skills is one example where 'training overspill' occurs. This benefit is itself a problem when the same staff are involved in mentor training for ITE students, NQTs and appraisal of colleagues when these courses are uncoordinated by the agencies involved. More specifically these key people may well be involved in a mentor training programme from each of the HEIs the school is involved with. Since much of this training is generic rather than course specific, it makes sense for such training programmes to be regionally accredited. This will enable mentor training provided for schools to be recognised across HEIs.

Given the nature of mentor training and its potential role in staff development for individuals and groups, some form of accreditation seems essential. In such schemes credit could be given for involvement in mentor training and mentoring, contributing to credits towards a higher degree.

● *Primary and secondary school differences*

AS HMI point out (DES 1991, paragraph 5 vii):

The organisation of primary schools and the small size of them, together with the heavy teaching loads undertaken by most primary teachers, mean that they do not generally have the capacity or the range of expertise needed to take on significant additional training responsibilities without considerable support. Secondary schools are better placed than primary schools to take on additional training tasks.

The subject based organisation of secondary schools can facilitate their subject specific training role whereas the class-teacher based primary school can militate against the development of particular subject expertise so important in developing the beginning teacher and meeting the subject knowledge and application competence criteria expected from CATE.

● *Roles and responsibilities*

A clear definition of the roles and responsibilities of those involved in ITT is a prerequisite to effective partnership. There are difficulties, as we have seen, in relying too much on documentation, important though this is. Part of the role of the Faculty-based mentor/tutor must be to recruit and induct the teacher closest to the student during their school experience. This time and effort is front-loaded and repaid by reduced level of direct supervision during the latter part of the school experience.

Students need to work alongside successful and experienced teachers working on activities planned by teachers and also those planned by students. The student also needs to observe a variety of teaching approaches and also to have opportunities to try these out on their own with a full-class. The balance between these opportunities will be dependent on student, course and school contexts, but unless the partners have a clear understanding of their respective and complementary roles — misunderstandings and confusion can arise with many missed experiences and opportunities for professional development.

In this debate on partnership between HEI and schools the role of a key partner, the ITT student, is often neglected. If ITT students are to act responsibly and autonomously then the ITT experiences need to prepare the student for this role. Involving the ITT student more actively in their own development is critical in this regard. Some of the competences needed take a long time

to develop fully e.g., critical self-appraisal of classroom performance, reflexivity, etc.

The use of the competence-based approach and professional
development profile with its regular self-review targets and action
plans will help. A recognition by HEIs and schools of the need to
acknowledge the role that students (only) can play in their own
professional development and learning extends the partnership into
what HEIs and schools can do *for* (rather than to) the developing
teacher. In doing this we are sending important messages about the
centrality of the learning process. Clearly the role and responsibilities need clarification, not only in terms of shared understanding
based on good will, but as a partnership agreement which acknowledges both the professional context of such training and the need for
clear statements of who does what, when, in relation to course
management, delivery assessment and evaluation. Definition of
these respective functions provides a basis on which to ensure that
appropriate resources are provided and allocated.

- *Schools are not directly resourced for training teachers*

Whilst this is true for most of the students trained from
September 1993 it will not be true for all of them. Two hundred and
fifty primary and secondary PGCE students will be trained in a
consortium of schools in the South East of England (validated by
Roehampton Institute). £1,000,000 will be provided directly to the
consortium by the DFE. The consortium can 'buy in' from HEI *if* it
decides this is appropriate.

Other funded institutions include the OU PGCE scheme for
1,000 students, again on both primary and secondary routes to
Qualified Teacher Status (QTS) beginning in February 1994. In this
scheme students will nominate a school for training; convenience
rather than suitability serving as a selection criterion. £1,000 per
school is being offered by the OU to take part. The National
Association of Head Teachers (NAHT) is in close contact with the
OU regarding the development of this course.

The funding of school-based schemes of teacher training in the
HE sector has been negotiable on an individual HEI/schools basis.
At present the 'going rate' is about £800 for the twenty four weeks in
schools. This figure is arrived at by negotiation with schools in
relation to the school's role in the course, and what the HEI can
afford when central administration costs and course costs are
covered. A school taking three to five students would receive
£2,400–£4,000 for their teacher trainer needs. In the main they
would be used to provide cover for mentor release in supporting
students.

A debate as to whether this is adequate continues — my guess is it depends on the course structure, who is asked to do what, the calibre of the students and the extent to which schools feel they are being asked to do much more than they already do.

Schools also need to acknowledge the value of closer association with an HEI and contact with HEI staff as course members on a more regular basis. Some schemes also build the CATE renewal of school experience (ROSE) requirements into their schemes. This effectively provides several days of supply cover in the school. In short, whilst funding is important to schools struggling with the implications of LMS, the overall package on offer needs consideration rather than the 'bottom line' cash transfer.

Implications of school-based training for mentors

The development of school-based ITT undoubtedly puts much greater emphasis on the role of the teacher who supervises the students within the school.

> The central role of teachers in initial teacher training is the supervision and guidance of students in schools. (DFE 1991, paragraph 44)

Given the moves to increased school-based training and the CATE criteria, we can add the mentor's role in assessment to those of supervision and guidance.

Under existing course provision those who most closely mentor students are given little training, time or acknowledgement for their efforts. Despite these handicaps the mentor–student relationship is most often a positive, personal and professionally beneficial one, particularly when mentors are successful and experienced teachers who serve as models.

Mentor-teachers have detailed information on schools, children and other staff to pass to students if their school experience is to develop curriculum coherence and continuity. Teachers in schools are best placed (by virtue of knowledge and location) to support students in their preparation, teaching and evaluation of children's learning. The faculty tutor is too often distracted from the central concern with learning, by classroom organisation and control issues. It is the continuing presence and support of the mentor-teacher which provides the best access to student understanding of chil-drens' learning — and their own professional development. There are particular problems in secondary schools where students have to establish themselves in relation to many more teachers.

The pattern of school experience can be significant in the mentor role for serial (rather than block) experience where time is limited calls for a more tightly structured programme of support.

The mentor–teacher role in assessment causes some role ambiguity. The open-hearted and self critical stance necessary for professional growth can be compromised by the role mentor-teachers have in 'student assessment'. Many of us would be reluctant to 'open-up' on our self-doubts and professional weaknesses if we felt it would influence the assessment by our mentor. We also need to remember that in this context assessment can mean the difference between passing or failing and getting/not getting a job.

The role of the mentor

The CATE notes of guidance accompanying DFE in Circular 9/92 suggest that schools will have a leading responsibility for:

— Training students to teach their particular subjects
— Developing their understanding of how pupils learn
— Training students to manage classes and to assess pupils
— Supervising students in relation to school-based elements of the course
— Assessing student competences in subject application and classroom skills

The role of the mentor is defined by the role that schools are intended to have in the training process. Furthermore this role will be established and set out in the partnership agreement between HEIs and schools with an annual statement to include details of the supervisory responsibilities of teachers (and tutors). It follows that mentors will need:

— An understanding of the partnership agreement and the arrangements underpinning it
— To ensure that the responsibilities relating to school induction of students into specialist subject teaching, how pupils learn, classroom management and the assessment of students are understood *and* in place

It also follows that mentors will need preparation to fulfil these roles and that this will best be achieved by the course team (tutors and teachers) developing particular skills appropriate to their distinctive roles in training.

Skills for mentoring

In general mentors will need to:

— Be experienced and competent, reflexive practitioners
— Have high-level interpersonal skills
— Be a high status member of staff in order to gain student access to whole-school support
— Be committed to the scheme
— Understand the personal and professional needs of students in training (working with adults calls for different skills than those gained by teaching children)
— Be open to the opportunities for their own personal/professional development

These sorts of people are likely to be already recognised for their skills and commitment and to be fully employed because of this. Mentoring students is not an 'add on' activity; space and time will need to be created. The transfer of funds from HEIs to schools is intended to create a mentoring system which is 'built in to the school development plan rather than bolted on'.

More specifically mentor skill training programmes will need to embrace;

— Classroom observation
— Advising students in terms of practical teaching and linking classroom practice to reading/study
— Target setting and negotiation of targets based on professional development needs
— Over-all management of the learning experiences of the student which need to be sequenced and progressive rather than *ad hoc*
— Establishing and maintaining a close and mutual trusting relationship with the student

Training for mentoring

Training for effective mentoring needs to be seen as a process rather than an event. There will be a need for 'kick start' training to embrace aspects of the role which are course specific on the one hand and generic (e.g. classroom observation, counselling) on the other. Beyond this there is a need for a programme of mentor development which forms part of the course. Scheduled and regular meetings between partners within the partnership; students/mentors, mentors, mentors/tutors on a regular basis to discuss and develop the course which will be dynamic since contexts (time, schools, mentors) are in constant flux. These developments are best determined by the partners themselves, based on agreed needs, rather than set out in a prescribed form. Such a flexible arrangement distinguishes professional from mechanistic approaches to mentor training and development. In the secondary school, particular attention will need to be given to the training needs of the subject mentor as well as the professional mentor who has responsibility for the scheme and all the students in training within the school. One problem in this context may be the need to train different subject mentors year on year as the subject specification of the students changes. In the primary context the importance of early and close involvement of the class teacher mentor is emphasised in all the evaluations of the Articled Teacher schemes. 'Arms length' mentor training is much less effective since the primary class-teacher working with the student will have a very hazy idea of the scheme, its expectations and demands. As HMI point out:

> Secondary teachers are no less busy than primary, but the way secondary schools are structured and organised makes it more straightforward for them to absorb trainees and offer them a breadth of experience. (DES 1991, paragraph 34)

Conclusion

> A consistent find over some years from inspection is that the overall quality of training is not a direct product of the amount of time spent in schools or of a particular pattern of school experience but rather the quality of the teacher and of the relationship between schools and training institutions. (DES 1991, paragraph 37)

The teacher-mentor has a pivotal role in the quality of initial teacher training. The significance of this role will be increased as teacher training becomes more school-based. As HMI observe:

> There is increasingly strong evidence that the designation of teachers as mentors or teacher-tutors, together with the provision of training, improves both their understanding of their role and the quality of the supervision they provide. (DES 1991, paragraph 73)

The future teacher force deserves no less.

3 Mentoring and newly qualified teachers

Malcolm Wall and Pauline Smith

Introduction

In this chapter the authors — an LEA Adviser and a HE Lecturer — demonstrate the value of a partnership approach to the mentoring of newly qualified teachers. The importance of building on a tradition of competency-based profiling introduced through the Articled Teacher Scheme is highlighted and issues in the design and delivery of both NQT and mentor training programmes are discussed. The chapter ends with an evaluation of the 'ideal induction programme' and reviews the design of the LEA professional development profile.

This chapter provides case study evidence of the value of an LEA/HE partnership in facilitating continuity of support and development through competency-based profiling and mentor training.

Developing a new approach to ITT — the articled teacher experience

The development of a competence-based approach to the induction of newly qualified teachers in Tameside LEA owes much to the earlier experience of an innovative and challenging approach to initial teacher training, the Articled Teacher Scheme. In describing the recent work with newly qualified teachers and mentors the relevance of this earlier experience cannot be over emphasised.

The Secretary of State for Education in his speech to the Society of Education Officers on the 27 January 1989, whilst welcoming the progress made by higher education institutions to extend the amount of time spent by students in school during their initial teacher training courses (ITT), indicated he wished to see further development of the principle of school based training.

Following consultation with teacher associations, higher education institutions and local education authorities some experimental programmes were proposed by the DES for school based initial teacher training, to be known as Articled Teacher Schemes. In essence the schemes were to be funded from the Local Authority Training Grants Scheme (LEATGS) for 1990–91 (DES Circular 1989) and required LEAs and ITT institutions to prepare joint bids to the DES for funding and to CATE for PGCE course approval.

The partnership between Crewe+Alsager College of Higher Education (Crewe+ Alsager College of HE) and Tameside Metropolitan Borough Council (Tameside MBC) developed as a response to the articled teacher initiative in ITT. The LEA and College viewed the proposal as an opportunity to develop an initial teacher training course which:

1. Placed students in school for 80 per cent of the two year PGCE programme and thereby enhancing their classroom and whole school experiences (DES Circular 1989)
2. Supported students in their PGCE training programme by the use of experienced school-based teachers trained as mentors and thereby also offering to mentors an important professional development opportunity
3. Defined the knowledge, understanding, skills, attitudes and qualities required of teachers by using a competence based professional development profile in the training and assessment of articled teacher students. (Crewe+Alsager College of HE, 1990)

The DES confirmed, in December 1989, the joint LEA and College bid for LEATGS funding had been successful and temporary course approval was awarded in 1990 following the submission of the course proposal to CATE. There followed, in a quite compressed timescale, further consultations with the professional associations in Tameside and a report describing the scheme and the costs was presented to the Education Services Committee (ESC Report, 1990). Throughout the planning process it was acknowledged that in order for the articled teacher scheme to be implemented in Tameside schools, the support of the Education Services Committee, the professional associations and schools was essential and the level of consultation and dialogue reflected this.

Within this supportive context, the recruitment of the first cohort of 15 students for the two year PGCE course began late in the Spring term. At the same time all the primary schools in the Borough were circulated with information about the scheme and headteachers were invited to express an interest in participation, after consulting with the governing body and staff. From the responses the base primary schools were agreed and, following interviews, five school based mentors were appointed, trained and allocated students for the first cohort of articled teachers who joined their schools in September 1990.

Sharing a philosophy and an understanding of mentoring and competences

From this summary of events it is clear that the experience of the Articled Teacher Scheme has been an influential one in Tameside LEA. In the three years from 1990 nearly 30 per cent of the primary schools in the Borough have had an articled teacher placement for a significant period of time. Articled teachers have worked with at least two class-teachers in each of the base schools and nine experienced class-teachers have held mentor appointments in this time. As part of their wider training programme articled teachers have also worked with high schools, special schools and pupil support services on project placements for special educational needs and multi-cultural education. Finally, the first cohort of articled teachers completed their two year course in July 1992 and six of the cohort were subsequently appointed as newly qualified teachers to primary schools in Tameside, some in permanent posts, others on temporary contracts.

In the context of a competence based approach to the induction of newly qualified teachers the articled teacher experience has provided valuable insights for the LEA and its schools. Perhaps the most significant are:

1. The value to be obtained from working closely with one higher education institution in a real partnership with clearly defined roles and responsibilities (Boon 1992)
2. The role the LEA can play in partnership with its schools to co-ordinate and facilitate new initiatives which, because of their complexity, benefit from sharing, rather than narrowing, ideas and professional support in the process of implementation
3. The importance of dialogue, training and support for mentors and class-teachers in the development of a shared understanding of the 'language' of a competence-based profile and in the

achievement of consistent judgements in the process of professional development and/or assessment

4. The challenge of reconciling a competence based approach to ITT, and all the preconceived notions professionals may bring to the term 'competence', with the need to make the process of assessing the student's progress through the competence profile manageable and professionally credible

5. The significant investment of time, money and professional expertise made by all the partners in the programme and the need for on-going support for mentors, class teachers and students (Boon 1992)

The successful implementation of the articled teacher scheme in Tameside schools undoubtedly gave the LEA, Crewe+Alsager College of HE, and very importantly, the schools themselves, the confidence to embark on the development of competence based approach to the induction of newly qualified teachers. The imperative to do so came from a decision at national level about the future of the probationary year for newly qualified teachers.

The last of the 'probationers'

The Secretary of State for Education announced, in July 1992, the abolition of the statutory period of probation for newly qualified teachers (DFE 1992). The significance of this statement, following on a period of consultation begun in September 1991, lay in the timescale for implementing the decision. It meant the end of the period of probation for all newly qualified teachers taking up post from the 1 September 1992. This decision was not totally unexpected given the inclusion of a new initiative in teacher induction under the Grants for Education Support and Training (GEST) funding.

Tameside LEA had developed, over a number of years, an induction programme for probationary teachers new to schools in the LEA. Since 1988 the programme had been funded from external grant and it was a well resourced in-service activity. Many of the aspects of the guidance published by the Department for Education in August 1992 (DFE Administrative Memorandum 2/92, 1992) for the 'Induction of Newly Qualified Teachers' had been part of the induction experience of probationers in Tameside schools for some years.

However, the implementation of GEST in the 1992–93 financial year placed great pressure on activities previously funded under the Local Authority Training Grants Scheme (LEATGS) from the local priority category (DFE Draft Circular 1991). The induction of probationers was one area of activity to suffer from the financial pressure and subsequently the residential element and the opportunities for a probationary teacher to be released, using supply cover, to attend off-site inset or to visit other schools were much reduced. The introduction in the GEST Draft Circular for 1992–93, published in August 1991, of Activity 27 — Induction Training (DFE Draft Circular, 1991) was seen by Tameside LEA as an opportunity to build upon the experience of the Articled Teacher Scheme and to enhance the support for newly qualified teachers. The criteria in the DFE Circular made it very clear that the funding was

> . . . to enhance the quality and organisation of induction training, contributing to the recruitment and retention of newly trained teachers, by initiatives to integrate initial teacher training and induction; co-ordinate the induction activities of LEAs and schools; and develop differentiated provision to meet the needs of individual new teachers. (DFE Draft Circular 1991)

and therefore the activity area should be used to encourage new developments related to competence-based Professional Development Profiles for NQTs and links with higher education initial teacher training programmes.

The LEA's bid to the DFE for grant under Activity 27 — Induction Training was the result of negotiation with Crewe+ Alsager College of HE and the objectives included:

1. A commitment to quality and coherence in the induction of NQTs
2. A partnership between the LEA and senior managers in schools to ensure quality and coherence in the observation, guidance, support and assessment of NQTs
3. The introduction of a professional development profile with a commitment to the use of a competence based approach to the professional development of NQTs

The bid did not envisage large scale resourcing for the induction programme and of course, the assessment element was overtaken by events and the decision of the Secretary of State. It was a matter of concern that the development should be manageable, provide value for money and very importantly, remain possible when GEST funds were withdrawn. The LEA's experience of other projects funded from LEATGS and, more lately, GEST grants indicated that a degree of caution was needed in order to implement a quality induction programme which was not dependent for success upon continued high levels of funding.

The programme submitted to the DFE for Activity 27 established priorities and timescales which in September 1991 seemed sensible and achievable. The decision in July 1992 to end the statutory year of probation and the anticipated publication of DFE Circular 9/92, in late June defining the competences expected of NQTs for ITT (secondary phase) caused the LEA and the College to revise the timescale. It was felt that it was particularly important for work with mentors and the production of the competence profile to reflect Circular 9/92. The LEA had to acknowledge that work planned for the summer term would have to move into the autumn and the profile would be delayed. As an interim measure, head-teachers in all schools in the LEA were sent, in early September, information about the revised arrangements for the 'assessment' of newly qualified teachers and an outline of the developments planned for the induction of NQTs under GEST Activity 27(92).

Newly qualified teachers — the way ahead for induction

The first stage of the revised programme was to invite newly qualified teachers to a 'Welcome to Tameside' meeting in October. This was an opportunity to meet their school's pastoral adviser and, although the Professional Development Profile could not be made available, it was possible to describe the elements the profile would cover and the level of in-service support they could expect as NQTs. The second stage of the programme was to invite all schools where an NQT had been appointed to send the member of staff with responsibility for NQTs to a preliminary half-day meeting in November 1992. The half-day session was designed to provide opportunities for consultation, discussion and mentor training. The process allowed teachers to discuss and define their perception of the mentoring role for NQTs, to be introduced to the *Mentoring — Core Skills Pack* (Acton R, Kirkham G and Smith P, 1992) and to start the process of designing a professional development profile with a well defined set of competences to support the induction of NQTs.

From the outset the work with mentors and NQTs was under-pinned by four important principles:

1. The induction of NQTs had to be seen as a continuum involving — initial teacher education → induction → teacher appraisal → further professional development. The coherence of an individual teacher's experience was therefore seen as a priority
2. In an LEA the size of Tameside it is not very efficient to attempt to operate phase-specific training for mentors or NQTs where generic training is appropriate. The opportunity for sharing

creative idea across the primary and secondary phases has been
one of the successes of the work to date

3. The process is seen as genuinely consultative and the views and
experiences of mentors, NQTs, headteachers, LEA staff and
HE staff have been invaluable in the construction of the
competence profile and the design of elements of the mentor and
NQT training programme

4. The induction of NQTs is important enough to invest a
significant amount of the time of professional staff from schools,
the LEA and HE in a dynamic and on-going process of
development

The action plan which resulted from the meeting with mentors in
November in 1992 envisaged:

• The preparation of a professional development profile for NQTs
with a competence based format; and
• The design of a training/development programme for NQTs and
mentors in the Spring term

Launching the professional development profile

In November, the mentors were offered a draft profile document
which owed many of its features to the LEA's experience of the
Articled Teacher Scheme and Crewe+Alsager College's PGCE Student Profile. The range of competences was greater and the draft
sought to tackle the issue of a profiling as a normal part of a teacher's
professional development. This proved a good starting point for
discussion at the meeting and the limitations of the draft document
became very apparent as the debate went on.

The opportunities presented by the competences were acknowledged but the group was concerned about the language and style of
the early draft and it was generally felt the profile could be more
useful if additional sections were included to extend the 'professional
development' element of a profile. At this early stage the shape of the
PDP began to emerge in terms of personal information an NQT
would find useful to hold in one document; for example, qualifications and previous experience. This is followed by an opportunity
for an NQT to record term-by-term a commentary and self-
evaluation of their first teaching experiences. The PDP is viewed as
an on-going process and to this end, provision is made in the profile
to record teaching experience beyond the first year and to set this in
the context of a personal record of professional development and
inset opportunities. The decision to include a direct link to the
process of teacher appraisal in the section 'Using the Professional

Development Profile' was taken to support the principle of the continuum from ITT to induction and on to further professional development.

To make progress and to capitalise upon the mentors' enthusiasm for the task, written comments and views were sought from all mentors, after consultation with colleagues in their own schools, and a small working group agreed to meet in twilight time in December to re-draft the profile. As a result of the comments, it was possible for the working group to undertake substantial work on the language and style of the competences. The most significant work was to change the rather formal descriptors into more user friendly questions. It was felt the lightening of the vocabulary, combined with asking questions rather than a checklist of descriptors would make the profile professional and humane, enabling the language of the competences to reflect the developmental nature of the process the Professional Development Profile was to support.

Some examples of the way in which the broad competence statements taken from Circular 9/92 (DFE, Circular 9/92, 1992) have been converted into manageable and understandable questions may give something of the flavour of the PDP (Tameside MBC/Crewe+ Alsager Faculty, 1993). The statements in bold are from Circular 9/92 whilst the italics illustrate the questions the working group devised to enable each of the competences to become more real, and in some senses more manageable, for the NQT:

6.2 Subject application

Newly qualified teachers should be able to:

6.2.4 set appropriately demanding expectations for pupils:
- *Do you match and differentiate work according to the individual needs of pupils in a given context?*
- *Are you aware of special educational needs including those of the more able pupils and do you plan appropriately?*
- *Do you have high expectations of and for your pupils?*

6.2.8 demonstrate ability to select and use appropriate resources, including Information Technology:
- *Do you try to manage and organise settings and resources efficiently and sensitively — e.g. furniture, space, materials, audio visual aids, information technology?*

6.3 Class management

Newly qualified teachers should be able to:

6.3.2 create and maintain a purposeful and orderly environment for the pupils:
- *Do you start and end sessions/lessons efficiently and effectively?*
- *Do you plan and organise your time efficiently?*
- *Do you pace and time your lessons effectively?*

6.4 Assessment and recording of pupils' progress

Newly qualified teachers should be able to:

6.4.2 judge how well each pupil performs against the standard expected of a pupil of that age:
- *Do you know the level an average pupil of the age range in your class is expected to achieve?*
- *Can you use this knowledge to balance against the particular circumstances of your pupils?*
- *Do you recognise the effects of teacher expectations and assessments on pupil achievement? — see 6.6.7*

The working group made good progress in December and a second draft of the PDP was thus available for all the mentors to comment on by early January 1993. After some minor modifications it was generally agreed that we had a profile document which would support the training/development programme planned for NQTs and mentors in the spring term.

Even though a substantial amount of progress had been made because of the commitment of a very professional group of teachers, it remained important to keep reminding all concerned that the process of developing the PDP was not complete. The programme for NQTs included a review day late in the spring term and the PDP would be subject to development in the light of the experience gained by NQTs and mentors of the process of using the PDP.

Delivering the Mentor/NQT training — issues arising

The opportunity for the same two trainers to design and deliver both the mentor and much of the NQT programme of development is one of the major strengths of the Tameside experience and clearly puts into practice the principles of communication, collaboration and coherence identified in chapter 1. The fact that both trainers had considerable experience in the 'competences' and 'profiling' served to ensure a commonality of language and purpose which helped to bridge the divide between HE and LEA which can sometimes exist.

At this point it may be helpful to the reader to share some of the detail of the training programmes devised for Professional Mentors and for NQTs in Tameside and to share some of the issues in the design and delivery of such programmes which are then taken forward in the final two sections of the chapter.

Contracting with clients is a well versed field of testing out perceptions of need and expectation; yet every trainer knows that it is virtually impossible to ensure that perceptions have been shared fully until the training event begins! The first mentor development event did not differ from this common experience and participants arrived with differing expectations and knowledge bases in terms of 'what is mentoring' but with an open willingness to engage in discussion about the 'role of the mentor' (stimulated through the card sort activity described in chapter 4); and moreover the value of 'competences' and 'profiling' — which surprised the HE partner who had met considerable reistance elsewhere at the mention of the term! This willingness to engage in debate and 'to have a go' has been one of the positive features of the development work in Tameside and must have a direct relationship with the 'hands on' experience gained by a significant number of teachers through the articled teacher scheme referred to earlier and through the permeating culture of competency-based profiling which is now clearly in evidence.

The objectives for this first Professional Mentor Training event were wide-ranging and ambitious in the time available, i.e. one half day session (see Figure 3.1). Most of the time was taken up with sharing the knowledge and understanding of a mentor's role and responsibilities and the role of the Professional Development Profile in the NQTs development; agreeing the value of a skills based approach to mentor development and planning a way forward. There was little time available in this session to start the skills development work, but there was general agreement that the next session should be devoted to this area of development. Several members of the group volunteered their services for the twilight/ independent working sessions that were essential to ensure that Tameside's own NQT profile was produced in the short amount of time available and once again demonstrated their professionalism, collegiality and stamina in a period of change and overload. This first mentoring event had achieved three out of its four objectives.

The Mentor/NQT training events were organized so that they were both 'alternating' and 'joint' — that is, an NQT training day in January 1993 followed on from the Professional Mentors' session in November 1992; this was followed by a Mentoring Skills Development session for mentors in February and by NQT training in

Manchester Metropolitan University

Crewe + Alsager Faculty

Mentoring Training

for

Professional Mentors at

Tameside LEA — Wednesday 25 November, 1992

Objectives

- To share knowledge and understanding about the role of mentoring

- To enhance the skills involved in mentoring through the use of the Core Skills Pack

- To investigate the use of a draft profile for NQTs

- To identify further development needs and to devise a programme for Spring/Summer

Programme   (Tea will be available during the afternoon)

1.30 p.m.   Welcome and Background to Mentoring Developments

1.45 p.m.   Examining the Mentoring Role — an activity and discussion

2.25 p.m.   Diagnosing the Skills of Mentoring — Introducing the Core Skills Pack: Self reflection and Discussion

2.45 p.m.   Professional Development Profiling and the role of competences — Input and discussion

3.00 p.m.   Developing the Skills of Mentoring — Session (1)

3.45 p.m.   Identifying further development needs Action Planning

4.00 p.m.   Close

Figure 3.1 Crewe + Alsager Faculty Professional Mentor training course

March. At the end of each NQT day, i.e. from tea onwards the mentors joined the NQTs for the final activities of the afternoon.

The advantages in this structure are considerable in terms of continuity and planning. The trainers were able to share the perceptions of the NQTs regarding 'what had gone well' for them in school to date; and also to discuss with mentors in their follow on session some of the 'areas of difficulty/for further development' identified in mixed groups by the NQTs. Anonymity and sensitivity was thus protected, with all its attendant advantages and disadvantages for real change. A compilation of the views expressed by 60 NQTs towards the end of their first term of teaching can be seen below.

Areas of difficulty/for further development

- Finding work/tasks to match ability levels
- Handling mixed age classes
- Coping with assessment and record keeping
- Relationships with parents
- Relationships with staff
- Quality control of work — are the children really trying?
- Time for readers and chances for 'quality' individual chats
- Curriculum co-ordination
- Discipline
- Involvement in 'whole' school
- Display and providing a stimulating environment
- A positive regard for *all* children
- Contact with parents
- Classroom support for SEN pupils
- Classroom support for E2L pupils
- Differentiation
- Record keeping — masses of paperwork
- Time management — seen to be *always* working
- Relationships: staff, children
- Encouraging parental involvement
- Lack of professional support
- Opportunities to observe other reception teachers at work
- Sending children home wearing incorrect clothes
- Assessment/record keeping
- Hearing readers
- Discipline — needs to be more structured, consistent
- Displays
- Prioritizing
- Lack of support from senior management

- Problems with other members of staff — lack of communication/ politics/personalities
- Planning work according to ability
- Discipline — getting children to listen
- Professional pressure
- Having too much planning in detail
- Mixed ability teaching
- Keeping children on task when working in groups
- Teaching PE
- Interesting classroom lessons
- Strategies for teaching mixed ability
- Mentor system
- Keeping up with admin/assessment marking
- Lesson planning/evaluation
- Second subject — not qualified
- Allowing the job to take over
- Too attached to pupils
- Not meeting the needs of mixed ability groups
- Teaching pupils who cannot read or write (TESL)
- Feeling de-skilled
- Need more support from form tutors of difficult pupils
- Too hostile with kids
- Have become less assertive (within departments etc.)
- Being drawn into confrontations with pupils
- Inconsistency in discipline
- No time or motivation to try new ideas

Successes/Achievements

- Better relationships with most of the children than expected
- Classroom organization
- Most display work has been interesting
- Planning has been thorough, but easier
- Relationships with parents
- Relationships with staff
- Good relations with most of the children
- Increasing confidence and learning from mistakes
- Involvement in 'whole' school
- Providing stimulating environment
- Learning value of praise
- Getting up
- Not as stressful/time consuming as TP — therefore a social life!
- PE (Primary)
- Building good relationships with children and staff — to varying degrees

- Support from other staff
- Autonomy within the classroom
- The role of the form tutor
- Relationships: staff, parents, children
- Successful PE lessons
- Team teaching
- Children's attitute to writing
- Creating stimulating environment
- Planning/preparation
- Retained a sense of humour
- Reduced overdraft
- Relationships — parents, staff, children (with exceptions)
- Curriculum planning and preparation
- Children enjoy work set
- Relationships with children
- Well-prepared — classroom management and organisation
- Good support from other members of staff
- Children enjoying thematic work/PE lessons
- Relationship with pupils better than expected
- Planning — successful
- Time management — mixed
- Extra-curricular activities
- Relationship with tutor group
- Relaxed atmosphere
- Some 'problem' pupils have now settled down
- Survived!!
- Feedback from parents
- Coping with running the department — due to staff being absent
- Role of form tutor
- Relationship with head of department and rest of staff
- Motivating year 10 class
- Motivating children

It is not surprising to find that the 'Mentor System' in school was identified as both a 'success' and an 'area for further development' across a wide range of primary and secondary schools.

The benefits of mentors joining with NQTs for some very limited training, in terms of time, were apparent to all involved. One of the major recommendations from the interim evaluations in March identified the value of a full session of Joint NQT/Mentor training and this is now planned for July with the focus of 'Managing Stress'. It should be a fruitful session! One of the disadvantages of joint sessions must lie in the negative effect for NQTs when their Professional Mentor is not able to attend the joint session — for valid reasons, of course; but nevertheless the message for the NQT and the importance of their professional development is not a positive one. Fortunately, this happened rarely and there are strong signs of a culture of expectation in joint training taking place which mirrors some of the best practice in joint appraisee/appraiser training.

The training for both NQTs and mentors has also been organized on a cross-phase basis. This has provided economies of scale; but moreover has helped to break down some of the artificial barriers that exist across primary/secondary. It has provided a positive role model for professional development for the teacher at the start of their career to be able to explore and share common perceptions and experiences with a new teacher from another phase and to appreciate the overlaps! Similarly, Professional Mentors from primary and secondary have expressed appreciation of the benefits to be gained from cross-phase work. The often highly developed interpersonal communication skills of the more informal small primary school is complemented by the formally and planned induction programme of support shared by secondary colleagues during discussion.

Discussion and sharing of experiences has proved to be one of the major benefits gained from the training sessions to date for NQTs. They valued practical, problem-solving activities in small groups (sometimes phase-related); and did not want anything they had already had at college!

One of the group activities that fulfilled this criteria was part of the March programme where the NQTs were posed the following 'problem' . . . or rather 'challenge' . . .

• You are the SMT in school. In September you will be taking on five NQTs; they will be joining five different departments.
    1. Discuss and agree a *Plan* for the induction of these NQTs over the year
    2. Draw up a *Job Description* for the Mentor(s) in the school.

Note: this brief was amended to *two* NQTs for the primary groups.

The detailed induction programmes designed by these NQTs is included in the next section. They reveal the clear demand for a structured framework of support/an entitlement for the NQTs professional development and a strong desire to clarify the roles and responsibilities of a mentor. In other words, the activity revealed the advantages inherent in the formalization of an NQTs programme and the unanimous desire for structured and planned time set aside for classroom observation, discussion and target setting.

It is interesting to note that the same views were expressed by the Professional Mentors one month earlier in their 'targets for further development' and the intention expressed by several that they would formalize the more casual approach that had previously taken place.

It is also not surprising that amongst these 'action plans' were the targets to 'negotiate more specific time to support the NQT'; and 'to organize myself better in order to spend time with the NQT'.

Time–Time–Time is identified consistently by mentors as a support strategy they would like to receive. Time to spend with the NQT (a joint weekend residential was suggested); time to educate the whole staff; to devise an induction programme for new staff and in-post induction for all staff; to revamp the staff handbook; and time to develop the competences — to widen them to include existing teachers linking this to concepts of regeneration and motivation. Quite clearly, the Professional Mentors see mentoring as a whole school activity; make links with appraisal; and, see mentoring as an essential part of the on-going professional development of all teachers.

In relation to their own professional development, the mentors expressed the strong desire to carry on meeting and sharing experiences with other mentors (which requires time!); and, the desire to extend skills in the areas of observation feedback and interviewing skills. A limited amount of this skills training had taken place through the half day sessions for both NQTs and mentors both separately and finally delivered together in March 1993. A videoed PE lesson was used for observation purposes against the class management competences within the PDP and the giving and receiving of constructive feedback skills were practised within a very short amount of time! NQTs were encouraged to take on the role of mentor in giving the feedback to the Professional Mentor who willingly role played the PE teacher. The use of trios helped observation and reflection of practice at the end of the activity. This openness and willingness to debate the issues frankly on both sides of the mentoring partnership has consistently been in evidence in the Tameside development work this year.

There are many issues surrounding the use of competences in teacher development. However, Tameside teachers have demonstrated their willingness to see the advantages in sharing explicit criteria with NQTs; and have seen the need to make the Competences of Teaching identified in Circular 9/92 more accessible and user-friendly, for use by constructing questions for self evaluation purposes and as an agenda for discussion between mentor and mentee. This positive approach does not infer, however, that in Tameside there is an uncritical acceptance of the value of competency-based profiling.

An interim review by mentors in February 1993, revealed the intentions of the mentors to monitor the use of the PDP; to provide support to NQTs in the use of the PDP; to arrange for NQTs to use it together; to talk about it together; and to invite NQTs to comment

Brief — using the PDP (1)

- *Read:* Section 4 — A Record of Professional Development Opportunities
- *Complete:* The Record of Professional Development Opportunities — using this training course as an example of a professional development course or activity and *in discussion with your mentor*

Personal record of professional development opportunities

This section of the profile can be used to record important information about your on-going professional development as a newly qualified teacher. The record can be extended as your career progresses to:

- include significant experiences which form part of your professional life as a teacher and link these to your involvement in the process of teacher appraisal

- record experiences which can be accredited as prior learning for further professional qualifications by higher education institutions: and

- help you with the completion of application forms and letters

The format below offers a way of recording important details:

Course, programme or activity title

Format of the course, programme or activity

Date/s

Qualification obtained and awarding institution (if applicable)

Course/Programme Provider

Outcomes and Action Planning

Figure 3.2   Using the PDP (1)

on the effectiveness of the PDP both generally and specifically in order to consider whether the time investment is really worth it! The issue of continuity of support and coherence of practice across institutions and LEAs was also discussed by Professional Mentors, who are well aware of the increase in temporary contracts for NQTs because of the pressure on school budgets.

Several mentors expressed the view that the PDP should be extended (in principle) to other staff and could see the value in an ongoing record of achievement process for themselves. The training activities in 'Using the PDP 1 and 2' had perhaps helped to formulate this view (see Figures 3.2 and 3.3).

All mentors wished to engage in further training, preferably jointly with their mentee, as mentioned earlier. The limitations of GEST and devolved budgets inevitably make this an increasingly difficult task for the LEA to manage effectively. In this scenario, it is helpful to know that mentors were pleased to receive a copy of the Core Skills Pack produced by Crewe+Alsager Faculty and that early evaluations reveal an intention to further develop mentoring skills and 'to become confident by reading the skills pack'. The authors of this chapter feel sure that further joint engagement in the skills based activities by mentor and mentee will follow on from this year's development work.

Brief — Using the PDP (2)

- Consider your *Previous Experience* — i.e. any work experience (voluntary or paid): or any qualifications obtained prior to teaching

- *Discuss* your prior experiences and achievements with your mentor and share the *skills* and *qualities* you developed through this experience

- How have these experiences/skills helped you as a teacher?

- As a result of this *discussion with your mentor*, take a few notes that will help you to complete this section of your PDP

Figure 3.3   Using the PDP (2)

Professional Qualifications

                    Award   Date of Award

Degree:

Diploma:

PGCE:

Other Relevant Qualifications

Type of Award (Certificate/Diploma etc.)

                                        Date of Award

Previous Experience

You may find it useful to record in the space below your previous experience of working with children, other employment and other qualifications which you think could be relevant to your development as a newly qualified teacher. This section is probably best tackled in two parts after a discussion with your mentor:

i)   a description of the experience, work or qualification with an indication of the dates/length of time involved;

ii) an analysis of the knowledge, skills and qualities you think the experience, work or qualification enables you to bring to your work as a newly qualified teacher.

Please add more pages if you need the space

Figure 3.3 *Continued*

Evaluation and review — issues arising

The review day in March with NQTs and Mentors provided both valuable insights into current practice in schools for induction and stimulated some creative thinking about the way forward for future work.

The experience of NQTs suggests there are shared understandings about mentoring, induction support, and competences but considerable variety exists in terms of an entitlement an NQT might expect as part of the induction process to their new school (OFSTED, 1993). The DFE Administrative Memorandum *Induction of Newly Qualified Teachers* (DFE 2/92, 1992) provides a framework for good practice, as do publications from professional associations (NASUWT, 1993) and the GTC *The Induction of Newly Appointed Teachers — Recommendations for Good Practice* (Calderhead and Lambert, 1992). Nevertheless, the experience in Tameside suggests, the role of the mentor is crucial in ensuring such principles and well-constructed guidelines are put into practice as part of a structured induction programme for the support and development of NQTs.

In attempting to analyse the experience and qualifications which may best fit a teacher for the role of mentor there is some agreement that an optimum of five-years teaching experience is about right with recent experience of teaching a similar age group or within the same key stage. Perhaps, most understandably, NQTs identified the capacity to empathise with what it was like to be a newly qualified teacher as very important for any potential mentor.

In a similar way, NQTs have been able to define some of the qualities a successful teacher would possess in order to best fit them for the mentoring role:

- Enthusiastic and committed, able to balance realism and idealism
- Friendly and approachable, with an outgoing personality
- A sense of humour
- Honest and frank, tempered by sensitivity

The choice of these qualities is closely related to the range and complexity of skills mentoring can demand:

- Being a good observer and listener
- Able to manage constructive feedback and to reflect on and offer realistic strategies
- Having good inter-personal skills and the ability to maintain confidentiality

Given the range of tasks faced by mentors, the balance of

experience, qualities and skills they can bring to the role is important. The review day with NQTs and Mentors offered an opportunity to design the 'ideal induction programme' and the section which
follows represents a distillation of the key elements of such a
programme.

1. In the period before taking up post

Access to an induction pack including copies of:
— the teaching timetable and curriculum/other school policies
— the brochure for parents
— the school policy on pupil assessment
— the school development plan
— the school procedures and regulations, particularly school rules,
   procedures for registers, dinner money and form teacher/class
   teacher responsibilities
— duty rotas and routines
— a plan of the school building/s
— the names and responsibilities of teaching and non-teaching
   staff
— subject area/department schemes of work
— teaching resource lists and where to find resources
— planning outlines and record keeping procedures
— the staff handbook/teacher file (which may include some of the
   above)

NQTs identified a range of people who could help them in their
preparation for their new post. These included:

— existing class teacher/s
— key stage teachers
— subject co-ordinators
— department staff
— the 'NQTs Mentor'
— teachers who were recently qualified

The NQTs wanted to spend time in school before taking up post:

— to talk to existing class or subject teachers about work to be
   planned from the NQT taking up post
— to observe classes around the school and shadow experienced
   teachers with an emphasis upon developing strategies for the
   management of the classroom
— to join in with school visits
— to join in with Inset days and whole school planning
— to accompany teachers on home visits (where this was appropriate)

There was a general willingness to spend time in school, prior to taking up their appointment, in order to better prepare them for the new post. It was also seen as an important stage in developing a relationship with the mentor, exchanging views and sharing an understanding of roles and responsibilities.

2. The first term after taking up post

NQTs emphasised their need for regular access to their 'mentor' and suggested:

— protected time for joint planning and preparation with the mentor
— protected time for mentors to observe them teach
— protected time for discussion/evaluation/review and profiling
— following an observation mentors should provide constructive written and/or oral feedback, as appropriate

In addition to regular meetings with their mentors, NQTs believed wider access to people and other experiences in the first term was very important, including:

— opportunities to observe other teachers in the classroom, other subject departments or in other key stage classes
— observation of teachers in other schools, particularly with children of the same age group as those of the NQT's class
— regular opportunities to meet other NQTs in their own and other schools, the networking role of the LEA was seen as valuable
— support from experienced staff in dealing with difficult classes/ pupils and the first parents meeting

In order to succeed in their first post, NQTs described a reduced teaching/administrative role as a key issue and suggested:

— ensure protected/guaranteed non-contact time for observation, planning, preparation and work with the mentor
— avoid giving an NQT a form teacher responsibility or sharing the responsibility with an experienced teacher in the first term
— avoid giving an NQT a specialist subject/curriculum responsibility (in primary school) in the first year
— be sensitive timetabling (in secondary) to avoid difficult classes and heavy examination loads e.g. Year 11
— avoid giving an NQT cover duties or minimise cover duties in the first term (secondary)
— provide clarity and support in the requirements for record keeping and lesson preparation

3. Second and Third Terms

As the academic year progressed NQTs wanted continued and regular access to their 'mentor' and time for:

— joint planning and preparation with the mentor
— mentors to observe them teach
— discussion and the process of profiling
— observation feedback to be oral and written
— opportunities to observe other teachers teaching

The opportunities for NQTs to network remained an important issue and the facilitator role of the LEA was seen as valuable and constructive. In addition NQTs recognised that LEA wide off site opportunities could be very useful for dealing with a range of common or shared interests including:

— the use of classroom display
— preparation for SATs, GCSE and pupil assessment, recording and reporting
— practical strategies for classroom management
— career advice and guidance

The issue of developing the whole school role of the NQT within a supportive and positive framework remained a concern for most NQTs. Again the pressure of time and expertise was raised with some real concerns about:

— guaranteed non-contact time for observation, planning, preparation and work with the mentor
— sensitive timetabling (in secondary) to avoid difficult classes, heavy examination loads (Year 11)
— reduced cover duties (secondary)
— continued support in the requirements for record keeping and lesson preparation
— acknowledgement that being an NQT made life that 'bit more difficult'

The design and style of the professional development profile

The review of the induction programme provided an important opportunity for Mentors and NQTs to comment on the design, use and further development of the professional development profile.

Although the language used to describe the competences had

been looked at quite rigorously by the working group, the review identified the following as development issues:

— work is needed to make the competences more 'user friendly' with clearer and more precise language in a number of the statements of competence
— areas of overlap and repetition between competences need to be reduced
— the overall complexity of the competences section could be reduced by using a system of indexing and numbering

The process of using the profile was described as generally helpful and positive. The evidence it helps to record about professional development is welcomed by most NQTs, as is the process of reflection which the profile combined with effective mentoring seeks to encourage. There were specific development points made about the style and design of the profile document:

— The majority of NQTs and mentors had some concern about the methodology for recording comments alongside the statements of competence, and it was felt an increase in the space for written comments would be useful together with a system for dating the comments
— The descriptors 'confident' and 'concerned' were felt to be too narrow and even negative: NQTs and mentors suggested the recording continuum needed to be flexible and positive in order to support the process. Suggestions for the continuum included:

  • a range of 1 to 5 with 1 as 'highly competent' to 5 as 'needs further attention'
  • an ungraduated range with 'highly confident' at one end and 'needs further development' at the other end

Following the review the revised PDP will provide an 'open' recording continuum with space for dating comments. In the notes of guidance for using the PDP some suggested descriptors for the recording continuum will be offered and NQTs can agree with their mentors their preferred option.

In general NQTs and mentors found the profile a useful tool in promoting the process of reflection and review of the development of a newly qualified teacher. Interestingly, there was some feeling that a prioritisation of competences would be useful to demonstrate which should be regarded as more important in the first term, for instance. Revised guidance notes about using the profile may help the NQT start the 'process of reviewing competences' and deciding with their mentor which of the competences should be the early focus for target setting in the first term of their appointment.

Where to next?

The development in Tameside LEA of a revised induction pro-gramme supporting the use of the Professional Development Profile and a competence approach to induction is set to continue with the intake of NQTs into schools in September 1993. There are several action points for the future to ensure that the progress to date becomes embedded in systematic good practice:

- The partnership of Crewe+Alsager faculty and the LEA needs to be sustained. The LEA is funding through GEST the NQT programme for the 1993–94 academic year and the faculty has submitted an evaluation report to the DFE to seek further support for continued work in the development of PDPs and mentoring programmes
- The schools in the LEA, working in partnership with LEA advisers and Crewe+Alsager faculty, will be encouraged to develop models of good practice for the induction and mentoring of NQTs as part of their entitlement to opportunities for professional development
- The opportunity for accrediting the NQT and mentor prog-ramme will be explored in 1993–94 to offer teachers the possibil-ity of building this substantial inset experience into a modular diploma or Masters programme course
- The professional development profile will be revised in the light of the experience in 1992–93 and changes to the design and structure of the competences section will be incorporated to reflect the comments of NQTs and Mentors
- A revised LEA co-ordinated induction programme will be offered which incorporates where possible, the suggestions of NQTs. Mentors and NQTs will be offered opportunities to work together in off-the-job training situations, funded from GEST in 1993–94

The experience gained of using a competence based approach in the Articled Teacher Scheme over a three year period and during the 1992–93 academic year for the induction of newly qualified teachers confirms the value of a competence based professional development profile and partnership between HE and LEA. The approach offers teachers in training and, more particularly, newly qualified teachers a supportive framework within which the knowledge, understand-ing, skills and attitudes required of competent teachers can be clearly understood, interpreted and put into practice. The process of the professional development profile can enable newly qualified teachers to identify with a mentor the further support, guidance and opportunities they need to build upon their initial teacher education experience. It also offers a degree of professional continuity for all NQTs, including those faced with temporary appointments and short term contracts, informing their entry into the appraisal system, and focusing self reflection on their own wider professional development.

4 Mentor training and development

Ray Acton, Pauline Smith and Glynn Kirkham

Introduction

In this chapter the authors provide insights into the mentor training programmes designed and delivered by HE lecturers during the academic year 1992–3. The value of the partnership with LEA, through GEST and DFE project-funded work, is also considered and the chapter ends with a summary of the major management issues raised through the training sessions and beyond.

The training framework — building the partnership

The most effective training framework is that based upon the foundation of the school–LEA–Initial Teacher Education (ITE) institution partnership. Such a partnership has long existed in order to facilitate staff development in the third stage of career progression (*viz.* the post-induction period) — while two partners (school and ITE institution) have worked together in the first stage (initial teacher training — ITT). The second stage, the induction period, was for long the concern of HMI, the LEA and the school. However, this stage has been radically changed by central government moves:

1. The issuing of Administrative Memorandum 2/92 (DFE, 1992) which laid responsibilities for newly-qualified teacher (NQT) monitoring upon LEAs and development upon schools, working to suggested criteria

2. The publication of DES Circular 9/92 which set out the competences to be attained by ITE students up to the point of entry into maintained schools
3. The publication of the Grants for Education Support and Training Circular (1992–3) in July 1991 to 'enhance the quality and organisation of induction training . . . to integrate initial teacher training and induction and to co-ordinate the induction activities of LEAs and schools'. Up to 40 LEAs were to receive specific funding assistance, provided that a clear indication of co-operation with ITE institutions could be given. Annual performance indicators included 'the number . . . of NQTs in each LEA for whom profiles are available' and the 'number of teachers . . . who have been trained in the observation, guidance and assessment' of NQTs. Herein lay the major contribution to the identification of the mentor role and the attendant staff development needs.

It was apparent to all three partners that many of the skills required in mentoring NQTs are equally needed in mentoring ITT students and are invaluable in the schoolteacher appraisal system planned to cover the whole of the third stage of the induction (and, since Administrative Memorandum 2/92, the induction phase as well). Thus the mentor could become the key person in the development of the concept of a continuum of growth from initial training onwards — a process seen in its most tangible form in the professional development profile.

The need for training large numbers of mentors — principally in the first instance for NQT mentoring — became a major concern for LEAs in the spring of 1992. Five NW LEAs with successful bids in category 27/92 of GEST (92–3) had named the Crewe+Alsager Faculty of the Manchester Metropolitan University as a major (if not sole) linked ITT institution. All five had close ITT and first appointment links with the faculty, while one had a fruitful working relationship through the Articled Teachers Scheme. The faculty had for some time been placing a strong emphasis on a competence-based approach for its 1,000 ITT students. It set up a team of five tutors to work on a geographical basis with the LEAs. Following detailed discussion of the respective bids, it was agreed that:

1. The faculty staff would work with LEA staff in the planning and delivery of INSET for mentors and NQTs
2. The LEAs would support faculty publications concerned with mentor skill development
3. The partnership should work towards a competence-based approach to NQT development — an approach in line with that used in ITT courses and influenced by DES Circular 9/92

4. The partnership should consult and involve practising teachers in all its development work
5. The partnership network should be formally established through a series of one-day or half-day meetings at the faculty to exchange information, spread good practice and tackle common problems

In the first year of its operation (June 1992–May 1993), the programme was threatened by the sheer pace and pressure of change throughout the primary, secondary and HE sectors — the 'restructuring' of LEAs, the new responsibilities of schools, the focus on curriculum and assessment, the requirement to introduce and train for appraisal in schools, the growing number of 'non-standard' NQT contracts and the real costs of mentor time all conspired not only to increase the need for mentor skills but also to blur the focus on such development.

Nevertheless, the partnership — with its 300 schools requiring NQT mentor training — effected a programme of development which met the DES indicators (above). The factors making for a successful partnership would seem to have been:

1. Identification by LEAs and ITT institutions of individuals with a clearly defined responsibility and the involvement of practising teachers on the network group. This group of eight was large enough to be representative and small enough to be decisive
2. Recognition of existing good practice — in particular, the familiarity with the ITE competence-based approach, the experience of mentoring Articled Teachers, the widespread planning and introduction of professional development profiles and the techniques successfully employed in appraisal training
3. The production of training and guidance material, arising from and leading to further staff development activities *viz.*
    Mentoring — A Core Skills Pack (Acton, Kirkham, Smith 1992)
    A Guide to Mentoring in the Primary School — Competences and Issues (Kirkham 1992)
    and
    A Guide to Mentoring in the Secondary School — A Competence Based Approach (Smith 1992)
4. Close liaison, from the initial planning stage through to joint delivery and evaluation, between the ITT institution and the LEA, to produce an activity-based mentor training programme. Such co-operation was perhaps facilitated by the inclusion in the faculty team of tutors with very recent LEA and school experience. Such a programme is enriched by its being based both in the particular LEA (whereby local networks can be established)

and at the faculty on a regional or national basis (whereby good practices may be shared and wider networks established)

5. A clear recognition by all partners not only of the need for mentor skill development but also of the imperative for managerial development. Training sessions, using a short, faculty-produced booklet, *Mentoring: Management Implications*, have recognised the importance of the school's management of what may be a small army of ITT mentors, NQT mentors and other staff (some would say all the staff) who have mentoring functions

6. A recognition that, while there are broad shared strategic goals — for example, the need to work along the three-stage continuum through a competence-based approach, there are many different starting points; materials drawn from out-of-area sources already in use may, after evaluation, be seen to be well worth retaining, amending and developing. It has also to be remembered that schools receive both ITE students and NQTs from a wide geographical area and a variety of training approaches and experiences

7. A joint approach to the delivery and sharing the results of questionnaires which provide data about the mentor process in schools. LEAs collect data from all NQTs and the Faculty collects data from all those graduating in a particular year. The resultant evaluation findings should form a major item on the agenda of the partnership network

8. The formalisation of training as the mentor role develops. This entails a move beyond information-receiving and general skills practice into the recognition of wider management issues, in-depth skills training and the development of a training role. The sense of progression is best embodied through flexible modular accreditation of mentoring achievement, i.e. the gaining of 'points' which contribute to award-bearing courses such as the BA, MA or MEd courses

Designing the mentor training and support materials

The need to provide support to schools and their mentors in the development of mentoring skills and also to provide advice and guidance in the management of the mentoring process was clear to all partners in our local partnership.

Over the past year of the project development, this need has been partly addressed by:

- The production of flexible learning and training materials — the Core Skills Pack
- The writing of competency-based guides to managing mentoring in the school
- The designing, delivery and evaluation of programmes of mentor training and development at a national level and for the professional mentors in three out of five of the participating LEAs in the partnership

The **Core Skills Pack**, designed by the authors of this chapter was produced before the inaugural meeting of the Partnership in the summer of 1992. It concentrates on the development of those vital inter-personal communication skills of the mentoring process; and raises awareness of the roles and responsibilities of the mentor in school through the use of interactive materials.

The Pack covers:

- What is a mentor?
- Motivation
- Effective listening
- Effective observing
- Body language
- Reflexivity
- Giving and receiving constructive feedback
- Negotiation
- Problem solving
- Managing stress
- Using time effectively
- Target setting
- Evaluation chart
- Further reading

Most units are designed to allow both mentor and mentee to work through the skills-based activities together, using a collaborative approach to learning and stressing the appropriateness of the generic skills training for both mentor and mentee professional development. Each unit was designed with an input-interactive process — reflection/evaluation structure, thus providing the necessary knowledge and understanding of the skill or competency area; engaging the mentor/mentee in skills based activities; and then allowing a reflection or self-evaluation of the learning achieved through this unit.

An extract is provided here to demonstrate the structure and processes:

Giving and Receiving Constructive Feedback

Introduction

Feedback is information you give to people about their behaviour and its effect on you, how you feel towards them and what you want them to achieve.

Giving constructive feedback is therefore an important communication skill for mentors to use since it increases self awareness, identifies options for alternative behaviour and thus encourages development.

Both positive and negative feedback can be constructive or helpful if it is given skilfully since it identifies areas for continued or further improvement.

Mentors can also help mentees to give and receive feedback in a constructive way by understanding and sharing the process with the mentee.

Input

The Principles of Giving Constructive Feedback

Mentors should take care to:

- *be concrete and specific* say exactly what the mentee is doing and focus on specific behaviour
- *refer to actions and behaviour* say what the mentee is doing and what can be changed. Keep it impersonal
- *own the feedback* make statements instead of general comments of praise or blame
- *be immediate* be sure to give helpful feedback at the time it is needed. This is usually immediate but can also be at a planned time, a little later
- *be understood by the receiver* make sure that the person receiving the feedback understands what you are saying. Use your active listening skills.

Mentees can be taken through these principles by the mentor as part of their ongoing development as a teacher/tutor.

The Principles of Receiving Feedback Constructively

Mentees can be encouraged to receive your feedback in a constructive way by adopting the following strategy:

- *Listen* — don't jump to your own defence immediately. Give yourself time to make sure you are clear about what is being said. Try repeating the evaluation to check out your understanding
- *Decide* — whether the feedback is valid and helpful. You are entitled to reject the criticism, but remember that although feedback can be uncomfortable to hear, it is helpful to know how others see our behaviour

- *Respond* — decide how to act as a result of the feedback: how to use the criticism to aid your personal and professional development
- *Let go* — do not build up the criticism in your mind. It is often better to disclose how you feel about the feedback and the way in which it was given. Then let it go and move on

Constructive Feedback
Practise the skills of giving and receiving constructive feedback by:
Write down and analyze three feedback statements *you* have received in the last few days. Evaluate them against the criteria given. Were they helpful or unhelpful?

1		
2		
3		

If the feedback was unhelpful, practise turning the statement into constructive feedback.

Mentor/Mentees are able to use the units within the Core Skills Pack as a basis for building up a reflective portfolio relating to the competences of mentoring. This portfolio can then be used as evidence of achievement for further professional qualifications using a modular accreditation system of award.

Evaluations of the use of this pack across three LEAs and through national response to a TES advertisement, has confirmed the 'early' perceptions of the authors that this practical approach to mentoring fits the perceived needs of individual teachers and managers.

Providing a balance to the skills based approach of the pack has been achieved through the production of **Booklets** or **Guides** which provide information and discussion about the roles, responsibilities, tasks, selection and training and management issues surrounding mentoring in schools and colleges. These easy-to-read guides have, we are assured, helped the newcomer by unravelling some of the mystique surrounding 'competences', 'profiling' and 'mentoring' and thus provided support for the teacher, manager and many of our own in-service students writing in the area!

These support materials have been used in the design of the **Mentor Training Programmes** delivered during the past year on a national and a local partnership level. Collaborative planning by the authors produced a one-day course programme for mentor development which attempted to respond to the perceived needs of a wide-ranging group of course applicants.

The advertisement for the one-day mentoring skills development course had attracted applicants from a wide geographical area: Rugby, London, Cambridge, North Wales and more locally from Staffordshire, Cheshire and Manchester. The course participants were local schoolteachers and headteachers, both primary and secondary; nursing tutors; in-service students and ITT tutors from HE institutions as far afield as London. How to respond to a wide variety of experience and interest in mentoring (or preceptorship as it is known in the nursing world) in a one-day course proved a major challenge and resulted in the successful programme (see Figure 4.1).

Inevitably in a short course the balance between skills training and awareness-raising of the complex management issues involved in managing ITT and NQT mentoring must fall towards the awareness-raising end of the continuum. Tutor input, activity, group discussion and a case-study approach was used to raise understanding and stimulate issues for debate across phase, sector and even profession!

A closer examination of one of the activities designed to stimulate wide-ranging discussion may be of interest to the reader.

Examining the mentoring role was designed by the authors as a card sorting activity for use in a small cross-phase/sector . . . professional groups. Here participants were invited to share their views, experiences, understanding about the role of the mentor (the who, why, what, where and when of mentoring) through a discussion of the 'statements' on the individual cards. They were then required to make group decisions about whether they agreed or disagreed with the statement and to place it appropriately on the flip paper. Examples of the 'statements' are provided below:

- The best person to be a mentor is a deputy head
- A mentor is an assessor
- A mentor is a trainer
- A mentor is a role-model
- A mentor should always be a subject expert
- Mentoring should be a whole-school activity
- Mentors should be paid more
- There should be a check-list of competences
- Mentoring is like supervising student teaching experience
- Every teacher should have a Professional Development Profile
- Mentors need one hour a week with mentees
- The main task of the mentor is lesson observation

Manchester Metropolitan University

Crewe+Alsager Faculty

Thursday, 12 November 1992

Aims: *To bring together interested parties from the partnerships involved in mentoring*

Objectives:

*   To exchange views and understanding about the role of mentoring
*   To examine the value of mentoring skills and the means by which they can be further developed
*   To identify some of the key management issues in the mentoring process

P R O G R A M M E

09.30 a.m.   Welcome and Background to Mentoring

09.40 a.m.   Examining the Mentoring Role — an activity

10.20 a.m.   Diagnosing the Skills of Mentoring — self perception

10.45 a.m.   Coffee

11.15 a.m.   Competency based Mentoring — an approach — Input and discussion

12.00 p.m.   The role of the PDP — Input

12.15 p.m.   Lunch

13.15 p.m.   The Mentoring Situation in School — Analysis and discussion

14.00 p.m.   The Management Implications in Mentoring — Input, activity and discussion

15.00 p.m.   Target Setting — Individual and Institutional Action Planning

15.15 p.m.   Evaluation and Networking

15.30 p.m.   Close and Tea.

Figure 4.1 Crewe+Alsager Faculty – one day mentoring skills development course

- Mentoring is essentially dealing with problems
- Mentoring should promote equal opportunities
- Mentoring does not cost anything
- The mentoring process should be totally confidential
- The mentor must be a good classroom teacher
- The mentor should appreciate the value of educational theory
- Write in:
- Write in:
- Write in:

The activity revealed that there was strong agreement that the mentor should be a good classroom teacher (but not necessarily a subject expert) and considerable disagreement that 'the best person to be a mentor is the deputy head'. This is interesting in the light of the fact that the participants in the LEA mentor training sessions were largely deputy heads!

The discussion stimulated by these statements inevitably raised issues relating to the selection and training of the mentor back in school and of the skills and qualities that were valued by course participants through their own experiences in ITT and NQT mentoring. Participants placed great value on the inter-personal/communication skills of the mentor.

It is interesting to note that there was no firm agreement that mentors should be paid more! Yet, disagreement that mentoring does not cost anything. Indeed, there was strong agreement that mentoring should be a whole school activity and group discussions revealed perceptions of the need to educate the whole staff in the mentoring role; to formulate a whole-school policy on mentoring.

One other part of the course programme deserves further detail. **The Mentoring Situation in School** — analysis and discussion, entailed a role play by the course team. This represented a scene where the mentoring interview and its essential skills, qualities and management were definitely not in evidence! The role play was followed up by a group brainstorming of 'what had gone wrong' and these ideas were categorized in terms of individual and organizational issues. The authors felt the need to role-play this scenario (despite their limited acting abilities), since at the time of writing there is a dearth of video material for mentor development which exemplifies good and poor practice for use in training sessions — media publishing companies please take note!

The one-day course evaluations were most helpful in terms of our forward planning of the LEA based Mentor Development courses later in the year and issues relating to 'timing' were fully taken on board. Course participants had found the day valuable, stimulating with 'much food for thought'. They enjoyed meeting colleagues from other phases, sectors and other professions; participants were most keen to stay in touch with one another and with Crewe+ Alsager in terms of networking and were very keen to receive any further materials on mentoring.

The networking issue is one that ITT representatives in particular are very interested in and Margaret Wilkin in Cambridge University Department of Education has taken a leading role in promoting networking on a local or regional basis for school-based ITT developments, in order to share ideas, provide mutual support and quality training and to further the partnership between schools and HEIs. We like to think that our one-day course has contributed towards those aims.

Fired with enthusiasm and aided by an improved understanding of course participants' needs, a two half-day mentor training event relating to the induction of newly qualified teachers was designed and delivered in Wirral LEA. Again, there was a need to provide information and context about 'What is Mentoring' before skills training could meaningfully take place; and group discussions of the important management issues took place through the skills-based activities which focused particularly on negotiation, observation and feedback and target-setting skill areas (see Figure 4.2).

The training of approximately 70 professional mentors from across Wirral schools was organized collaboratively with Wirral LEA staff and funded through GEST; the sessions were delivered across-phase. Evaluations revealed the value of course members receiving the Core Skills Pack and Mentoring Guides at the end of the first session and thus being able to engage in some of the reading and activities before the next session. Several participants felt that the sessions could be improved by having the mentee present as well; for example, when discussing and practising negotiation skills.

Most participants found the two sessions of 'considerable value' and appreciated the opportunity to discuss in small groups. One or two members felt that the primary/secondary differences necessitated separate groupings for at least part of the training session. Most participants wanted more time and nearly all indicated the need for future sessions. Inevitably many participants felt that the training course should have been provided at the beginning of term, or earlier — rather than in late November/early January. (For a discussion of the time constraints involved in managing GEST 27 funding see chapter 3).

In both the one day and the Wirral LEA training sessions, **Competency-Based Profiling** underpinning mentoring was given an 'airing' — e.g. through the negotiation activity. The general level of awareness of its present usage and future value in teacher development was, however, perceived to be fairly minimal. ITT

Metropolitan Borough of Wirral —

Education Department

and

Crew+Alsager Faculty

The Induction of Newly Qualified Teachers

Mentor Training

Thursday 26th November 1992

Programme

1.15p.m.–1.30p.m.	Coffee
1.30p.m.–2.15p.m.	What is Mentoring? Activity
2.15p.m.–3.00p.m.	What are the mentoring skills? The mentor pack
3.00p.m.–3.30p.m.	Tea/coffee
3.30p.m.–4.10p.m.	Case study in mentoring
4.10p.m.–4.30p.m.	Plenary and evaluation

Thursday 7th January 1993

Programme

1.15p.m.–1.30p.m.	Coffee
1.30p.m.–2.25p.m.	Negotiating skills
2.25p.m.–3.15p.m.	Observation and feedback
3.15p.m.–3.35p.m.	Tea/coffee
3.35p.m.–4.10p.m.	Target setting
4.10p.m.–4.30p.m.	Plenary/Evaluation

Figure 4.2 Wirral MBC, Education Department two half-day mentor training courses

students may well have been profiling back in their education
departments for the past few years, but this practice has evidently
not made an impact during the school practice and neither has the
NQT asked for support from the school to continue her profile and
target-setting. Things are about to change of course and course
members did perceive the area of competences, profiling and target-
setting as areas for their own future professional development.

Issues arising from training

Language

The language used in mentoring needs to be consistent. While the
term 'mentor' is generally used for the experienced and supportive
person, there is a variety of terms used to describe the recipient of
the mentor's attention: protégé (used in much American text
(Daresh and Playko, 1992; Greenberg and Baron, 1993) which
suggests the role of mentor as being that of protector); 'mentoree',
which has a suggestion of linguistic correctness (GF Shea, 1992) and
'mentee', which is generally gaining currency (Acton, Kirkham and
Smith, 1992; Wilkin, 1992) and is the preferred term used here.

Selection issues

In order that the role of mentor to newly-qualified teachers is given
the important professional development identity which it deserves, it
is necessary for those who have the role to be well-respected as
exceptional teachers of children (pedagogues) as well as exceptio-
nally well-balanced and skilled androgogues (teachers of other
adults). Selection of mentors is, then, a matter not to be taken
lightly.

Matching-gender

One of the issues which arose as a question during training and
which concerns selection of a mentor was that of matching. While it
is important to recognise that the characteristics of a good mentor are
genderless, there is increasing evidence that gender-matching may
be helpful to the new teacher. It is recognised, of course, that in
some schools (particularly, small primary schools) there may be few
options. Some larger schools are adopting the approach of giving the
mentee a choice of personnel.

Matching-age

Matching-age was also an issue which was raised when considering the needs of the NQT. While a NQ young teacher may well be comfortable talking to another recently-qualified and, perhaps, equally young person (it is worth noting that as a result of the high numbers of unemployed persons and, for other reasons, there is an increase in the number of 'mature' — over 25-years old — entrants to the profession) about matters of common interest, it is unlikely that the slightly more experienced teacher will have either the network or the 'clout'/status to support the NQT as effectively as a considerably more experienced teacher. Much depends upon the individuals concerned and also on the size and phase of school. For example, in some secondary schools, the NQT may not be in the same department or even building as the recently-qualified teacher.

Role differentiation and clarification is also important in supporting the NQT. The mentor may be responsible for socialization and support, there may be other members of the school who are given responsibility for induction into the school or a department in the school.

Training needs analysis

It is also of importance that those individuals selected or nominated as mentors receive the training which is appropriate for the role they are to perform as mentors. In order that the training is directed appropriately, a training needs analysis for each individual mentor should be carried out. The analysis may initially be as simple as a self-evaluation against the skills required by a mentor along a graduated scale (adapted example from core skills pack). Evidence from the self-evaluation would then be supported by a similar evaluation exercise carried out by the mentor's promoter using the same instrument in order to provide a 'more objective' view of the mentor's skill capacities to date.

Findings from our own research on self-evaluation by teachers on the training programme would confirm generally-held views that some teachers (most often, women) tend to underestimate their degree of skill.

As a result of the analysis, a tailor-made programme of identified skills development should be derived.

There are skills which are common to both the mentor and the mentee (for example, listening and observing). It would make sense, therefore, to seek to enable such training to be available to both and, preferably, from the same deliverers and at the same time. The application of such skills are pre-requisites of those engaged either as mentor or mentee and being involved in the same training increases the bonding between the mentor and mentee.

It could be argued that all training both for mentors and mentees should be carried out with both parties present. Such an argument would, however, be failing to recognise the needs of individuals. There are issues which both mentors and mentees need to discuss in a forum which encourages honesty and openness at which frustrations on both parts may be vented. It may be appropriate, therefore, to receive the same input and then to break up into mentor groups and mentee groups.

Further, it takes no account of the very real 'power' which the mentor has relative to the mentee (who is a newly-qualified teacher — NQT — or, in the case of school-based initial teacher education/training, not yet qualified — NYQ), even though the mentor may not exploit the power that she/he has.

Planning

When schools know that they are likely to be employing newly-qualified teachers, from their forward-looking School Development Plan (that is, the data on teachers' age and likely retirement and other natural wastage factors) or as a reaction to a special circumstance (a long-term absence or a death of a teacher) leading to a teaching vacancy a mentor should be appointed and participate in skills development training.

Schools may wish to develop a group of trained personnel: in high schools, at least one in each department?

Costs

The decision to employ a newly-qualified teacher in a school has obvious financial implications, not the least being that, if the NQT is to replace an experienced teacher, there is likely to be a saving made on previous outgoing expenditure. Consideration of the needs and 'entitlement' (DES 2/92) of a newly-qualified member of staff may well require a considerable fraction of that saving.

Under LMS, much, if not all, of the formerly centrally-held funds for training have been devolved to schools (jam spread thinly) and, unless mentoring the NQT and the training for both mentor and mentee are seen as priorities as a part of the SDP, then money may not be available for training — many LEAs now charge for their services — or for quality time release from the teaching timetable with supply staff to cover.

The cost of not providing for such will be seen in:

1. Increased stress for both the mentor and the mentee, who will both strive as professionals to do their best to meet unmeetable targets
2. Reduced effectiveness in teaching and mentoring
3. A visible sign to all in the school of a lack of commitment to NQTs and the concept of mentoring

Partnerships

Schools and university education departments

It is imperative that the relationship between those who are to be mentors in schools and the HE institutions with ITT/ITE responsibility is not only maintained but increased if there is to be some form of continuity for the NQT and, for the mentor (and possibly other teachers), understanding of the course, its nature, purpose and content.

One practice, which is a feature of some initial training in HE departments of education, is the Professional Development Profile — a professional record of achievement, sometimes based on competences — which the student gathers from a variety of sources and which can point to strengths and areas for development for the beginning teacher. If continued throughout the life of the teacher, the profile can form a basis for discussion between the mentor and mentee (and, later, appraiser and appraisee). Here, again, the mentor can be supportive and act as a sounding-board for the NQT's own deliberations.

The mentor needs to have access to the information about the competences required of new teachers and how these are interpreted in practice. The work carried out by members of the Crewe + Alsager Faculty Education Department gives a detailed breakdown of current DFE competences and flushes them out into recognisable behaviour.

Local Education Authorities

The feeling of being isolated in one's endeavour can be destructive, especially when striving hard and seeming to make little progress. Such can be the experience of the NQT (which is one positive reason for encouraging the growth of mentoring as a supportive structure for beginning teachers). Mentors, too, can feel alone in the role that they perform. LEAs still, for most schools, remain the employer and as such have access to information regarding the nature and number of newly-qualified teachers in their individual authorities. As good employers, they would wish to ensure that NQTs (as a collective body) are welcomed into the authority and offered support at least during the first year of their new professional life. Some LEAs continue to follow this practice despite externally-imposed financial constraints, seeing such as part of the entitlement of the new employee.

It follows, then, that schools in partnership with LEAs can serve the needs of both the mentee and the mentor by, at the very least, furnishing schools with the information which tells schools where other NQTs are to be found and as a consequence where mentors are also likely to be found. From this data, schools may wish to join the parties together for, minimally, self-help groups. (MA classes — Mentors Anonymous). LEAs may see this minimum facilitation as part of their role.

Again, these activities need to be planned to obtain maximum effect.

Senior Management Teams could consider the following whole school issues in the selection and training of their mentoring partnerships:

Identify need
Identify potential personnel
Consider present workload of potential personnel
Remember school 'Pay Policy'
Discuss possibilities with potential personnel
Together examine role of mentor
Are there any other members of staff who are suggested?
Discuss possibilities with suggested staff members
Together examine the role of mentor
Remember school 'Pay Policy'
Come to a decision. (You may wish to ask the NQT.)
Allocate quality time in the timetable for observation and feedback and other regular mentor/mentee meetings
Effect a training needs analysis for mentor and mentee
Liaise with LEA/HE re courses available for NQTs and mentors
Allocate budgetary provision in SDP for appropriate training for both mentor and mentee
Link back to the HE institution for course details (and reference, if not already requested and received)
Ensure that mentoring is recognised as a whole school responsibility
Monitor the effectiveness of the process

In the *Induction of Newly-Qualified Teachers*, Calderhead and Lambert (1992) conclude with 14 points for progress which emphasise the importance of the mentoring process:

Schools:
1. There should be an explicit school policy for the treatment of newly-qualified teachers and school-based trainee teachers
2. Newly trained teachers should have an entitlement to extra non-contact time in their first year
3. There should be an agreed maximum pupil contact time for all teachers undertaking school-based training
4. There should be **designated non-contact time for professional tutors/mentors**

Employing authorities or other school networks:

5. There should be an explicit policy for the organisation's provision for newly trained and appointed teachers. This should set standards for schools as well as the organisation itself
6. A handbook should be provided for all newly-appointed teachers
7. *Training for mentors should be provided*
8. Information, training and support for returners and supply teachers should be provided
9. A code of good practice in the treatment of supply teachers should be drafted

All the partners:

10. All new schemes of school-based training should be monitored, with particular reference to the personal and financial factors that make for success
11. Research and development work, jointly between schools, LEAs and higher education, should continue on profiling/ competences
12. The current **training of mentors and operation of mentor** in schools should be evaluated and good practice disseminated

Government:
13. Government should ensure that the true reasonable costs of new schemes of induction, mentoring and school-based training are fully recognized in the global allocation of funds to schools

14. As new structures and roles in the management of education evolve, due consideration should be given to the
potential role of a General Teaching Council in the training
and induction of new teachers in England and Wales,
bearing in mind the Scottish experience

The quality of education in our schools has been repeatedly
demonstrated to depend heavily upon the quality of the teaching
personnel, their knowledge and skills and how these are managed
and supported within the school (Mortimore et al., 1988; Rutter
et al., 1979, quoted in Calderhead and Lambert, 1992).

As both secondary (1994) and primary schools (1995) take on not
only NQTs but also NYQs through school-based training, the
quality of education in our schools will increasingly be dependent
upon the quality of those who are engaged as teachers and mentors.
It is imperative, therefore, that those persons and their roles are
valued in and by their schools.

5 Mentoring in personal and career development

Pauline Smith and Joss West-Burnham

Introduction

In this chapter, the authors reveal the importance of the skills of self-review, target-setting and action planning in the personal and career development of teachers. The vital role of skilled and sensitive mentors in this process of career guidance for both male and female managers in the classroom and beyond is discussed; and the argument that mentoring can help to advance equality of opportunity for women's professional development in the teaching profession is explored.

What is personal and career development?

Personal and career development involves looking at the ways in which we can develop our personal effectiveness; examining where we are now and also working towards where we want to be in the future. Whilst this could mean another job, promotion or a career change, it could also represent the opportunity to develop within an existing role those transferable skills and responsibilities at present undervalued. These processes of personal and career development, involving self-review, target-setting and individual action planning can be greatly enhanced through the guidance and support of a skilled professional mentor in school.

Figure 5.1 illuminates this learning process and identifies the valuable role to be played by the mentor in personal and career development.

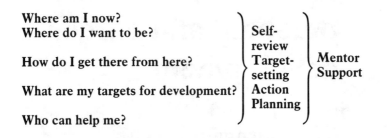

Figure 5.1   Personal and career development

Where am I now?

The need to be able to identify the skills, knowledge and competences demonstrated within our present jobs is paramount. This 'task analysis' allows a clearer picture of the job roles and responsibilities to emerge and perhaps a new job description to be agreed! It also starts the process of recognizing the value of those skills and achievements gained through the experiences of doing the job. A mentor can provide crucial support in this recognition process, through the affirmation of the value of the post or prior learning experiences and thus help to raise the confidence of the mentee.

Subject-specific or technical skills and knowledge are often the first to be identified in this job review process. However, it is the skills that relate to the way we communicate, solve problems and deal with other people — the 'transferable' skills — that are more important. These inter-personal skills are required across all dimensions of the teaching profession and do not become obsolete — unlike some parts of the national curriculum!

Competency-based profiling and portfolio building, where one is encouraged to reflect against particular statements or standards of competency and to gather evidence of achievement in those elements or units of competency, can be most helpful to the process of identifying subject-specific and generic skills. This method of reflection on career or management development through profiling can be NVQ (National Vocational Qualification) related and can be used to gain further valuable professional qualifications. The Institute of Training and Development Assessor and Verifier Awards are one example of the way in which teachers and lecturers can collect evidence of their experiences and achievements in relation to assessment and in so doing to gain NVQ related awards. The role of a mentor in helping the reviewee to recognize the value of their experiences and skills is well documented in competency-based profiling — see, for example, the School Management South competences referred to in chapter 1.

Using profiles to self reflect can therefore help to gain awards, but more importantly perhaps, specific statements of achievement (or, standards of competency) can help individuals to recognize their achievements in a detailed and positive way. There is considerable research available which demonstrates that women, in particular, have difficulties in recognizing the value of the work they do. A recent report by the South Australian Department of Labour found that the majority of the women interviewed '"invisibilised" their work by describing it in the broadest terms.' The report goes on to say that 'the most consistent feature . . . was the way in which the women minimised their skills and knowledge — repeatedly using words like "a bit", "just" and "only". This Australian research is equated with the experiences of British women workers, where despite Opportunity 2000, both women and the workplace consistently undervalue female jobs which are more likely to be in the human resource than the budgetary resource areas of work' (*The Guardian* 21.6.93).

A clear job description is therefore a vital tool in aiding self reflection and recognition of the value of the work done. It also forms the basis of an effective appraisal scheme; and is probably an essential element in performance related pay schemes of the future. It is clear that within the teaching profession we need to develop more highly the skills of analysing job tasks, roles, responsibilities and the transferable competences arising from achievement in these areas. A mentor can help in this developmental process through supporting the self review and helping the reviewee to identify transferable skills and to learn from past experiences. This of course requires competency in the guidance skills of mentoring as identified in earlier sections of this book.

The importance therefore of analysing 'Where am I Now?' lies in the opportunity to recognize what in our present jobs we enjoy and would like more of (and what we would like less of); and enables us to value our past achievements and strengths and thus to have the confidence to identify those areas for further development.

Where do I Want To Be?

The process of task analysis and self-reflection can help to formulate broad goals of personal and career development. These aims or ambitions are inevitably influenced by the level of motivation and self-esteem experienced by the person at the time.

There is some evidence to suggest that women in particular need help in the raising of self esteem. A mentor trained in the use of constructive feedback and target-setting can provide valuable support and help to increase the motivation of the teacher to apply for promoted posts. The figures available from DFE reveal that women have a 1 in 125 chance of becoming a headteacher, compared to 1 in 30 for men; and in primary despite the fact that 80% of employees are women that women have a 1 in 14 chance of reaching headship compared to a 1 in 3 chance for men (Khalifa 1993). These statistics reveal the wastage of female managerial talent that exists in the teaching profession and which show no real sign of improving.

There is further research which suggests that women tend to avoid applying for management jobs where management involves 'aggressive competitive behaviours, emphasis on control rather than negotiation and collaboration, and the pursuit of competition rather than shared problem-solving' (Khalifa 1989, p.89). Such behaviour is, of course, the antithesis of a mentoring culture of support and development which values using 'other people in positive and mutually supportive ways' (LM Segerman-Peck 1991). The introduction of a scheme of mentoring can therefore demonstrate and enforce the values of human resource management and investment in people argued elsewhere in this book, and can help managers to actively change the culture of the school to one of support for personal and career development.

How do I get there from here?

The twin questions of 'What are my targets for development?' and 'Who can help me to develop?' can be asked at this point in the learning process. Both questions when answered help to formulate an 'action plan' and thus facilitate the process of personal and career development.

By identifying those elements of the job that one enjoys and is good at it is possible, as mentioned earlier, to start to identify those areas requiring further development or change. These areas for development may refer to the working environment, relationships with colleagues or the dominant management style operating in school. The 'targets for development' to be set at this point, however, need to be achievable and very specific! These targets need also to relate to the subject-specific and generic skills identified earlier as being valuable skills transferable to any post in education and beyond.

The role of the mentor in helping the teacher to identify these specific targets for development and change is fundamentally important to this process of personal and career development and is central to a positive appraisal system.

In response to 'who can help me to develop?', this chapter is identifying and recognizing the central role of the mentor in the development process.

The following set of questions from Hennig and Jardim quoted by Segerman-Peck can be used to further clarify the role of the mentor in career development:

- Where am I now?
- What is my present level of knowledge, skill and competence?
- Who are the people I know?
- What positions do they hold?
- What can they help me with?
- What can they teach me?
- What information do they have that I need?
- Whom do they know who can help me?

(Segerman-Peck 1991)

Whilst the first two questions have already been considered; the last six questions give some insights into the role and purpose of mentoring and networking in career development.

Segerman-Peck provides some illuminating advice to women on 'finding and using a mentor', emphasising the value in both official and self-chosen schemes of mentorship as well as the benefit to be gained from having more than one mentor. Issues of gender, age, status and power differences need to be considered in finding or selecting a mentor; but perhaps the most important factors are concerned with the interpersonal or teaching skills that the mentor needs to possess, if they are to be of real benefit to the mentee in terms of further development or learning.

The benefits to be gained from a mentoring relationship are of course two-fold in terms of personal and professional development. Segerman-Peck identifies some of the 'employment skills' learned by the mentee from their mentors and groups them under the categories of: improving performance, technical skills, handling people, personal growth, career development and balance of home and career. These last three categories are worth recording here as they reveal the perceptions of women respondents on what they had learned with help from their mentors.

Career development

- Plan career
- Find out more about the job
- Make an impression at meetings
- Speak up at meetings
- Increase personal visibility
- Develop personal credibility
- Get new training
- Maximise training
- Transfer learning from one area to another
- Dress appropriately
- Understand company structure better
- Get promotion
- Increase power
- Increase assertiveness
- Recognise that personal humility may not be appropriate
- Increase influence
- Work the system

Personal growth

- Become aware of nutrition
- Develop environmental awareness
- Be proud of my accomplishments
- To move away from female stereotypes
- Enrich vocabulary, syntax
- Discuss feminist theory and history
- Become more confident
- Take responsibility for self
- Develop personal skills
- Become more assertive
- Remain within own personality but make progress
- Act with personal integrity
- Combat isolation
- Explore limitations of personal mindset
- Become interested in feminism
- Take interest in topics of the day

Balance of home and career

- Get perspective on job and career

- Obtain success without sacrificing personal life
- Cope with conflict of work and domestic responsibilities

Segerman-Peck notes that these lists reveal the job-specific nature of some skills identified, whilst others relate to the company environment, and yet others 'help the mentee to grow as an employee and as a person'. Mentors, as 'guardian angels' to their 'fledglings' as one organization refers to its mentors–mentees, offer help through the techniques of role modelling, protection, providing new learning opportunities, giving dispassionate feedback, sponsoring and recommending and having political knowledge and access to the informal network (ibid p.93).

Mentors with this level of competency and political awareness have been of direct help in getting women through the 'glass ceiling' — the barrier to promotion afflicting women at senior management levels. In the *Managerial Woman* written by Hennig and Jardim in 1979, the authors discovered that all of the successful women interviewed — that is, those who had reached presidential or vice-presidential levels in large companies — had had mentors who were also their line mangers. These mentors had guided and protected them, made sure they were seen as the right people for the next job and got them promoted.'These women went through the glass ceiling as if it didn't exist' (Segerman-Peck 1991).

More recent research by Arnold and Davidson (1990) in the UK has confirmed that both male and female managers 'found that their mentors were important for introducing them to the formal network of power relations which existed in the organization' (Davidson and Cooper 1992).

Networking, then, is identified as an important element in mentoring in most literature. The value of Round Tables, Rotary and the like have been clearly established within the male domain. Segerman-Peck refers to the value of the more informal networking-mentoring which she identifies as similar to 'peer-mentoring' where women of similar status mentor each other in a less structured system, providing support for career development in collegiate manner (op. cit. 1991).

Whatever the system of mentoring support designed, it is clear that mentoring is an important training development tool for the career success of both male and female managers. However, as Arnold and Davidson found there are some gender issues to be carefully considered. Their research in industry revealed that women are more likely to suffer specific relationship problems when mentored by a man; and that although same-gender mentoring may eradicate problems of stereotypical roles of sexuality, there are still very few senior female managers compared to males (Davidson and

Cooper 1992). It is interesting to reflect on whether the same gender
issues are important in mentoring in school!

Conclusion

In conclusion, the skills of self-review, target-setting and action-
planning are important in the personal and career development of
teachers.

It has been argued that mentors competent in inter-personal
skills and sensitive to the process of career guidance can play a vital
role in facilitating this development for both male and females, but
can substantially help to advance equality of opportunity for
women's professional development in the teaching profession.

The careful selection and training of mentors in these competences of mentoring is clearly indicated as is the encouragement of
reflexivity on the part of the mentee.

6   Mentoring and appraisal

John West-Burnham and Pauline Smith

Introduction

This chapter explores the relationship between the system of teacher appraisal in schools and the mentoring process. The appraisal regulations and circular are analysed to identify the management of a developmental approach to appraisal which is symbiotic to the principles and processes involved in mentoring in schools.

The chapter examines four components of appraisal: the appraiser/appraisee relationship; the structure of the appraisal process, the outcomes of the process and the relevant skills and qualities required. In each component the integral relationship with the processes of mentoring is established. The chapter ends with a summary of the value of incorporating mentoring principles into appraisal practices, and, the implications for management if 'appraisal as mentoring' is to be adopted in schools.

Exploring the relationship between appraisal as a system and mentoring as a process

The Appraisal Regulations provide a minimalist view of what must be done, they are largely silent on *how* it should be done. Circular 12/ 91 provides amplification of the Regulations but still leaves LEAs and schools with significant areas of discretion. This latitude provides important opportunities for the development of an appraisal system which is primarily concerned with learning. The generic aim of appraisal is to 'improve the quality of education for pupils, through assisting teachers to realise their potential and carry out their duties more effectively' (Regulations 4[2]).

This general aspiration is translated into more specific aims which may be summarised as:

- Recognising achievement
- Improving skills and performance
- Managing deployment
- Supporting career development
- Providing guidance and training
- Informing reference writing
- Improving the management of schools

These aims are potentially compromised in the Regulations by an indication that the outcomes of appraisal may be used in the context of decisions about pay, promotion and discipline. However, this potentially negative component of the Regulations is mediated by a number of factors:

(a) The outcomes of appraisal are developmental targets which cannot have a cash value placed on them, a quantifiable correlation is impossible

(b) The appraisal process is confidential and therefore information gained by appraiser cannot be divulged in other contexts. It could be argued therefore that an individual who is aware of the content of a teacher's appraisal should be automatically disbarred from involvement in pay, promotion or disciplinary procedures

(c) Disciplinary procedures are only relevant when appraisal has 'failed', the only linkage is a recognition that the appraisal process is no longer appropriate

If the integrity of appraisal is safeguarded by being 'ring fenced' from other personnel procedures then it is possible to produce a definition of a professional model which has the following characteristics:

- Developmental: concerned with learning and growth, not measurement
- Negotiated: a partnership based on mutual respect, not a control or power relationship
- Formative: analysis leading to action, not the imposition of judgements
- Anticipatory: emphasising the future rather than dwelling on the past

This view of appraisal is entirely consistent with the Appraisal Regulations and Circular 12/91 but it does presuppose a coherent view of professional development, sophisticated personal and professional relationships and a consistent staffing strategy. If this model is accepted then it becomes possible to establish the first links with mentoring. Shea (1992) offers the following definition:

> . . . mentoring is a process whereby mentor and mentoree work together to discover and develop the mentoree's latent abilities, to provide the mentoree with knowledge and skills as opportunities and needs arise, and for the mentor to serve as an effective tutor, counsellor, friend and foil who enables the mentoree to sharpen skills and hone her or his thinking. (p. 17)

There are a number of clear parallels between Shea's definition and the definition of appraisal proposed above. In essence both are fundamentally concerned with enabling and enhancing the individual. However, there is a fundamental potential tension in that whilst mentoring might be categorised as a process based relationship which is usually voluntary, appraisal is an organisationally driven activity usually defined in system terms and, in the case of teachers, a statutory and contractual obligation. It is therefore necessary to explore the components of the appraisal process to analyse the potential synergy between appraisal as a system and mentoring as a process and to identify the potentially dysfunctional elements.

Four distinct components of appraisal can be identified; the **appraiser/appraisee relationship**, the structure of the **appraisal process**, the **outcomes of the process** and the relevant **skills and qualities**. These same components form the vital elements of successful mentorship and its integral relationship with appraisal is explored in the following sections.

The appraiser–appraisee relationship

The Appraisal Regulations and Circular 12/91 make it clear that the designation of a teacher's appraiser is the responsibility of the headteacher. This requirement is amplified by the advice that appraisers should normally be the people who have a line management responsibility for the work of the appraisee.

This approach begs many questions. It assumes that schools have rational and functional hierarchies, it requires a clear definition of the responsibility of senior and middle managers in schools to manage the performance and development of their colleagues and it presumes credibility, trust and effective personal and professional relationships. It may be that in some schools not all these criteria are met. However, there is a very strong case for arguing that if senior and middle managers are not actively engaged in the development of their colleagues then why do they have differentiated status and pay? If teachers are a school's most precious resource then the function of managers must be to manage that resource. This implies that the primary responsibility of managers is to develop their colleagues. A process of inductive logic would lead to the conclusion that to manage is to appraise and mentor.

Segerman-Peck (1991) offers the following definition of the mentor:

> . . . (a) guardian angel. Someone who is knowledgeable, helpful, wise, prepared to help you along the path of your career, take you by the hand to help you over puddles in the road, catch you when you fall, and eventually give you the wings to fly alone. (p. 23)

Rather more prosaically Shea (1992) offers the following components of mentor activity:

- Set high expectations of performance
- Offer challenging ideas
- Help to build self-confidence
- Encourage professional behaviour
- Offer friendship
- Confront negative behaviour and attitudes
- Listen to personal problems
- Teach by example
- Provide growth experiences
- Offer meaningful sayings
- Explain how the organisation works
- Coach their mentorees
- Stand by their mentorees in crucial situations
- Offer wise counsel
- Encourage winning behaviour
- Trigger self-awareness
- Inspire their mentorees
- Share critical knowledge
- Offer encouragement
- Assist with their mentoree's careers (p. 18)

Smith (1992) has identified the following key words which interpret the role of mentor: trainer, developer, pedagogic counsellor, role model, coach, support, adviser, negotiator (p. 1).

By synthesizing these views of mentoring and linking them to the components of the appraisal cycle it becomes possible to establish linkages. Figure 6.1 demonstrates the intersections where there are particularly high levels of correlation. Obviously all the mentoring activities could be said to be relevant but there are areas which are particularly strong.

Mentoring	Initial Meeting	Classroom Observation	Self Appraisal	Appraisal Interview	Review Meeting
Setting Standards	X	X		X	
Challenging	X		X		X
Building Confidence	X	X		X	X
Encouraging Professionalism	X	X			X
Offering Friendship	X			X	
Confronting	X		X	X	
Listening	X			X	X
Providing Examples	X		X	X	
Providing Growth Opportunities	X		X	X	X
Offering Insights	X		X	X	
Explaining	X	X		X	
Coaching		X	X	X	X
Supporting			X		X
Counselling		X		X	X
Reinforcing Achievement	X			X	X
Raising Self-Awareness	X		X		X
Inspiring	X			X	
Sharing	X			X	X
Encouraging	X	X		X	X
Career Support	X			X	

X = a high level of correlation

Figure 6.1 The appraisal cycle — the relationship between mentoring and appraisal

Two important points emerge from these three perceptions. Firstly they are all entirely congruent with the developmental model of appraisal in that they describe a helping relationship which is proactive and concerned with outcomes. Neither appraising or mentoring are concerned with non-directive counselling nor are they an opportunity for the reinforcement of mutual ignorance. The Regulations and Circular do not offer a definition of the role of the appraiser but it is possible to derive one from the aims and activities central to the appraisal process:

> An experienced colleague who works as a critical friend to support analysis and reflection and helps develop strategies for improvement.

This definition creates the possibility of the appraiser as mentor. This raises the second issue — the possibility of this 'counsel of perfection' being attainable. Very few managers in schools have been appointed on the basis of their skills in working with adults. The problem is compounded by the notion of line management. It would be a happy school that had all its managers displaying the skills, knowledge and qualities implicit to this definition. Two responses are possible — flight and fight. Flight would involve 'hoping for the best', 'getting by', 'doing the best you can'. Fight (perhaps an inappropriate term) involves setting a standard and then training and developing staff to meet it. This also means that senior staff have to exemplify the principles in their own working relationships, i.e. training and exhortation are not enough, there has to be leadership by example. One of the most significant concerns of both appraisers and mentors is 'how to behave', the most powerful means of ensuring consistent practice is for the first mentor-appraisers to act as role models and so to set the precedent.

There is no incompatibility between the roles of mentor and appraiser and that of line manager; in many cases, they may be the same person. Indeed, these roles are mutually enhancing if there is a culture which sees management as being about on-going professional development, which stresses the importance of high quality interpersonal relationships and emphasises empowerment rather than control.

These whole school factors are very much under the control and influence of headteachers and senior staff and require a sensitive and knowledgeable approach to the roles, responsibilities and relationships of both appraisal and mentoring. Such an approach will recognize the benefits of a successful appraiser/appraisee relationship for both the individual and the institution and will seek to protect the 'outcome' benefits of appraisal through the 'process' benefits of mentoring.

The mentoring relationships involved in newly-qualified teacher induction and new headteacher mentoring have already been clearly established by the profession as being 'developmental' rather than 'judgmental'. Furthermore, the use of competency-based profiling for NQTs and managers, supported by DFE and DoE funding, is now gaining momentum and provides further support for the principles of empowerment and self-development identified earlier. It is argued that the incorporation of these developmental mentoring principles into the appraiser/appraisee relationship in school, can only serve to enhance and protect the benefits of motivation, recognition and professional development already evident in the first stage of appraisal implementation.

The key role for senior management, therefore, is to ensure that the roles and responsibilities of appraiser and mentor are clearly identified in terms of continuing professional development and that the vital relationship of appraiser/appraisee — mentor/mentee is protected by the careful selection and training of all staff involved.

The structure of the appraisal process

The Appraisal Regulations specify the components of the appraisal process: an initial meeting to set the agenda, classroom observation and data-collection, the interview itself and a review meeting. The circular endorses the concept of self-appraisal but stresses that it is not obligatory. The process occurs within a two-year cycle with the first three elements in the first year and the review meeting in the second year.

This model militates against the notion of appraisal for continuing development. The two-year cycle is totally divorced from the reality of school life where virtually every other management process is based on an annual cycle, e.g. curriculum deployment, INSET planning, the budget, etc. The statutory 'events' could create an artificial view that once the formal meetings have been completed then the responsibility for development is discharged.

The elements of the mentoring process can clearly be seen to be compatible with the components of the appraisal process (see Figure 6.2). However, the key element to be stressed in the mentoring process is 'continuing professional development' and the potential role to be played by competences in enabling a focused observation, feedback and target-setting to take place.

It is possible to argue, therefore that at present there is a potential tension between mentoring as a 'process' of continuing professional development and appraisal as a two-year 'system' of individual and school development.

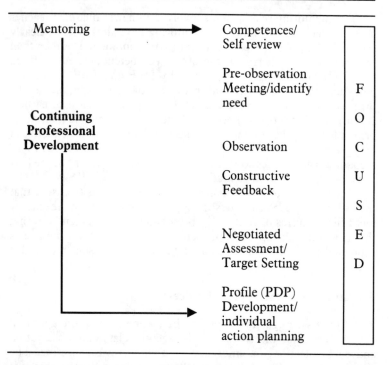

Figure 6.2 Elements in mentoring for professional development

We argue that this tension can be resolved if mentoring is seen as the key management relationship in professional development and appraisal as a more specific and formal component concerned with integrating the individual teacher into school processes, e.g. the school development plan, the INSET programme, etc. However, for this to work then the nature and purpose of each stage in appraisal has to be carefully defined and the key role played by mentoring firmly established.

The initial meeting

The main outcome of this stage is to agree the agenda for the particular appraisal cycle. However it should also involve clarification of the nature and purpose of appraisal and the respective roles of appraiser and appraisee. The formulation of the agenda based on principled is a good example of where the mentor–client relationship provides an effective model for the appraisal process.

There needs to be between two and five topics for review in each appraisal cycle; these topics are best derived from:

— the school development plan
— the appraisee's job description
— the appraisee's perceptions of her/his development needs
— the appraiser's perception of the appraisee

The emphasis is therefore on shared interpretation and focus through effective interviewing techniques; classic components of the mentor's role. At this stage the role of the appraiser is to help the appraisee generate an agenda which is appropriate, challenging and addresses real issues. It should also serve to motivate. The process is therefore one of disclosure of perceptions, prioritisation and negotiation of practical outcomes.

Once the agenda has been agreed then appraiser and appraisee need to agree the appropriate elements for classroom observation and further data collection; important elements in the mentoring process, used in the induction of NQTs and beyond.

Classroom observation and data-collection

This is the element of the appraisal process as defined in the Regulations which could be the most problematic as far as adopting a mentoring approach is concerned. The Regulations imply an inspectorial/assessment approach and this has led to the greatest apprehension on the part of teachers about being appraised.

However, it is possible to work within the Regulations and define this stage of the process so that it is consistent with a developmental/mentoring model. The shift required is from the appraiser observing/inspecting to the mentor understanding and supporting. If the agenda agreed in the initial meeting is sufficiently well focused then observation is in turn concerned with analysis of the teacher's performance in that specific context. The appraiser/mentor is gathering evidence to allow specific and detailed feedback which will inform review and eventually target-setting. In essence the process informs the mentor, helps to develop a common understanding, shared perceptions and, most importantly a shared language.

In order for this approach to work the following criteria have to be met:

— a clearly focused agenda is agreed
— the appraisee controls what is observed and when
— the 'behaviour' of the appraiser is agreed in advance
— methods of data-collection and recording are agreed
— there is immediate feedback

Throughout the process the emphasis is on the appraiser learning and understanding in order to help the appraisee.

The value of using a clear profile of teaching/management competences in the identification of specific and focused observational areas of development is, we would argue, fundamental to the process of negotiation and is supportive of the principle of empowerment which should lie at the heart of both mentoring and appraisal.

Self-appraisal

If the purpose of observation is to make the appraiser/mentor better informed then self-appraisal fulfils the same function for the appraisee. In essence self-appraisal enhances the appraisee's understanding of the topics under review and so increases the possibility of a partnership based on equal access to information and parity of esteem. A key function of both the appraiser and mentor is to facilitate the process of self-appraisal, this means developing techniques to support reflection.

West-Burnham (1993) identifies a range of strategies to help in the process of reflection and drawing conclusions to strengthen analysis. This process is parallel to observation and in a professional model of appraisal is equally, if not more significant. Few adults will be committed to learning and change unless they own the analysis and have a personal investment in the strategies for improvement. The notion of the appraiser facilitating self-appraisal helps to reinforce the movement away from an hierarchical/coercive model to one based on expertise and focused on development which lies at the heart of the mentoring process.

Self-review, using competency-based profiles, has become an established part of the development of ITTs and NQTs, underpinned by the need for an effective mentoring relationship. This process of support builds on the mentees' identification of need and ensures the raising of self-esteem and the recognition of real achievement.

The appraisal interview

After classroom observation the interview itself probably causes the greatest anxiety for appraisers and appraisees. A central concern is the nature of the relationship — in essence who controls the interview? Again mentoring provides appropriate and effective models. Shea (1992) encapsulates the relationship as the mentor 'recognising the needs of a person adapting to change and responding appropriately . . .' (p. 34). The potential of the appraisal interview to be a part of an effective long-term developmental relationship depends on two factors; the components of the inter-view and its management.

Three components of the interview can be identified:

1. Recognition and reinforcement of success
2. Drawing conclusions from observation and self-appraisal
3. Developing targets for development arising from the conclu-sions

One of the 'golden rules' of appraisal is 'no surprises' i.e. the appraisee has equal ownership of the agenda and outcomes. If there are perceived problems with the appraisee's work then these should be dealt with as and when they occur not 'saved-up' for the appraisal interview. This supports the principle of continuing professional development underpinning the mentoring process.

Positive reinforcement and celebration of success are as much valid outcomes of appraisal as the identification of development needs. This coincides with Shea's view of the mentor 'encouraging winning behaviour'. In the second stage of the interview the primary function of the mentor-appraiser is to help the appraisee draw conclusions about her/his performance by supporting the appraisee's reflective processes. The appraiser obviously contributes to this process; more by feedback and questioning than by *'fait accompli'* statements and subjective interpretation. Exactly the same principle applies to the generation of targets (see below).

The need for skills training in the active listening/questioning techniques of effective interviewing are, it can be argued, generic to both appraisal and mentoring, and indicate the possibility of cost-effective support and training being provided at whole school level.

The review meeting

This is perhaps the most artificial and bureaucratically inappropriate aspect of the Regulations. The notion of a single meeting twelve months after the interview is a triumph of administrative expediency over notions of effective management relationships and professional development. Effective appraisal and mentoring assume a continuing relationship not approximately 10 hours out of 2,530. There is a fundamental contradiction in the notion of a review every two years when most of the targets set will have a life-span of 6–9 months. The timetable for appraisal in the Regulations imposes an hiatus on development and militates against the integration of appraisal into a model of effective professional learning.

The concept of mentoring offers the practice of continuous development in which appraiser and appraisee use the appraisal cycle as the formal basis for review but superimpose it on a

continuing relationship in which target-setting and review are one of
the most important ways in which the management relationship is
expressed.

The outcomes of appraisal

The tangible outcomes of the appraisal interview are the targets
which help the appraisee to prioritise her/his work and development
needs. There is a danger that targets will be seen as synonymous
with 'going on courses' when all the evidence indicates that the most
powerful development takes place at work, i.e. by doing the job,
reflecting on how it is done and then planning for improvement. In
this context a mentoring approach is almost axiomatic to success.

The successful attainment of a target is much more likely if there
is sustained support available and there is a continuous process of
shared review and reflection. The strategies and techniques that are
appropriate at this stage of the process are discussed in chapter 1.
However, in the context of appraisal, specific issues can be identified:

1. If the agenda for the appraisal cycle is derived from the school
   development plan, the appraisee's job description and the
   perceptions of appraisee and appraiser then the targets need to
   be continuously managed in the context of the plan and the job
2. The appraisal targets are about improving aspects of the job —
   appraisal needs to be seen not so much as another thing to be
   done but rather as a better way of doing what has to be done
   anyway. This implies integrating appraisal into all aspects of
   management
3. The increasing requirement on schools to monitor and evaluate
   introduces a significant new element into the management role.
   The appraiser/mentor's involvement in reviewing targets to
   establish the extent to which outcomes have been achieved
   clearly presupposes direct and continuing involvement and help
   to fulfil the criteria for staff development within the OFSTED
   framework for inspection

The Appraisal Regulations could be interpreted as stating that
the appraiser's responsibility ends with the setting of targets and
only emerges again a year later at the review meeting. The notion of
the 'appraiser as mentor' model argues that the targets are a joint
responsibility and the continuing involvement of the 'mentor-
appraiser' is essential both to the achievement of the targets and is an
appropriate definition of the functions of managers. This integrated
mentor-appraiser role is as essential to the successful induction of the
NQT and to those staff new to their post as to the continuing

professional development of existing staff.

The selection and training of the mentor-appraiser is therefore a crucial management issue, vitally influencing the success of the process and the achievement of beneficial outcomes for both the individual and the whole-school.

Skills and qualities

This is potentially the least problematic aspect of the relationship between appraisal and mentoring. There is a high degree of consistency between a range of writers on the skills and behaviours which are appropriate to the developmental process. Shea (1992) identifies the following as 'particularly helpful' in the mentoring relationship:

— Visioning the future
— Listening
— Giving feedback
— Confronting negative intentions or behaviour
— Informing
— Empowering
— Generating solutions

Smith (1992) extends this list into a schools context:

— Subject knowledge and application skills
— Adult training
— Interpersonal and communication skills
— Monitoring and evaluation
— Problem analysis

These skills and qualities are paralleled by Trethowan's (1991) views on the 'key appraisal interview skills' which he identifies as: giving feedback, creating the climate for disclosure, active listening, asking questions and target setting. Trethowan stresses the centrality of these skills:

> As a result of a successful interview the organisation could have a teacher who feels that he or she matters to the school, that people at the school listen and care and that . . . he or she is being helped to develop personally and professionally.

> The appraiser can develop an appropriate attitude by putting into practice certain behaviours. These behaviours are expressed in detail as skills . . . (p.196).

Implicit to Trethowan's notions of recognition, respect, caring and development are the fundamental principles of mentoring that have been identified in this chapter.

The skills and qualities of appraisal and mentoring can be seen, therefore, to be consistent, generic and fundamentally important to the success of both process and system. The need for senior management to consider carefully the selection of mentors and appraisers in terms of their existing skills and qualities and their willingness to enhance or to learn new skills, for example in relation to adult learning, is paramount. Factors such as gender, age and attitude must enter into the selection process, alongside experience and expertise, and selection and training process needs to be managed carefully in order to ensure the establishment of effective learning partnerships in school. An investment of time is therefore required by senior management in order to ensure the on-going professional development of the mentor-appraiser and their respective partners in development.

Conclusion

This chapter has demonstrated:

- A high degree of congruity between a developmental model of appraisal and the mentoring process
- Parallels between the roles of appraiser, mentor and line manager
- Consistency between the processes in terms of skills and qualities; and, the potential value in adopting competency-based profiling
- Congruity between the components of mentoring and the stages of the appraisal cycle

Therefore, a professional model of appraisal and effective mentoring are symbiotic.

However, although it is possible to show high levels of commonality, the movement into 'appraisal as mentoring' presupposes:

- The roles of managers being defined primarily in terms of managing the development of colleagues
- Replacing the two-year cycle with a continuous process of review for development with the components of the appraisal cycle representing annual 'landmarks'
- Seeing the 'job itself' as the most powerful agent for professional development
- Senior management having the vision to invest time in the selection and training of 'mentor-appraisers', thus protecting the existing benefits of appraisal for both individual and institution

7 Mentoring and headteachers

Glynn Kirkham

Introduction

In this chapter, the author justifies the need for headteachers to have mentors. Drawing on the work of Daresh and Playko (1992, 1993) in the United States and their consultancy work in Britain, the skills of headship and headship mentoring are explored. Developments in headteacher mentoring are presented and recommendations for future action are propounded.

Mentors for headteachers?

> . . . at each stage of life and career, individuals face a predictable set of needs and concerns which are characteristic of their particular age and career history (Kram 1985).

Why should there be a need for headteachers to have mentors? After all, are they not in a sufficiently unique situation that, within a school, no one else is in a position to be the 'peer pal', 'guide', 'sponsor', 'patron' or even the parentalistic (neither paternalistic nor maternalistic but aspects of both) 'teacher' and 'advocate'?

In the course of this chapter, some answers to the first question will be proposed, some of the skills of headship will be explored as they relate to mentoring, some of the skills required of headteacher mentors will be presented, some developments in headteacher mentoring here and in parts of the United States will be presented, comments from headteacher mentoring in action and recommendations for future action will be propounded.

The chapter adapts and applies the leading developmental works of Daresh and Playko (1992, 1993) in the United States to the British experience.

Beginning heads

Headteachers in their first headship are, in fact, beginning head-teachers. In most cases, those who attain headship will most often have done so via the role of deputy headteacher and, although they will have performed a variety of roles delegated to them and thus gained valuable formative experience, they will not have experienced the full impact of responsibility for the day-to-day management of the school as well as its long-term future. There is a significant difference between being in the role of 'acting headteacher' and being appointed as the headteacher of a school.

In most British schools, the headteacher is not necessarily appointed from within the body of the school (that is, a deputy head of the school does not naturally succeed to the post). Currently, the post of headteacher is the only post which has to be advertised nationally when a vacancy arises. There are probably a good number of deputy headteachers who have 'seen off' a succession of head-teachers. Owing to the timing of resignations and the advertising and processing of applications prior to appointment, there are, of course, a number of interregna during which a deputy may be asked to assume the role of headteacher until a permanent appointment is made. That such is the case identifies a problem of continuity and progression for schools and highlights, perhaps, the need to consider succession planning and a school's development more seriously.

Even if the deputy has been 'acting headteacher' — an effective professional development exercise, and may, during an interreg-num, fulfil all the headteacherly duties, it is the case that where there is uncertainty about the future direction of a school there is a temptation to do little more than maintain the status quo. To act in such a way, it would seem, is a very reasoned approach to take since it would be foolish to set a school running in a certain direction when, in a few months time, someone new will come along and change that direction. It may be argued that, with definitive legislation regarding the purpose and curricular content of schools, the degrees of freedom available even to those permanently appointed as headteachers is severely limited.

It may be the case that a newly-appointed headteacher is already an employee of the LEA in which the school is sited. However, it is equally the case that a newly-appointed headteacher may be comple-tely new to the area. What then happens? Is she/he left to sink or swim? She/he also has to undergo socialisation into the new culture, the new environment and new relationships which may also accompany a house move and other stress-loaded factors.

Even when in a second or further headship, those newly-appointed to the post are still beginners in their new environment. The expectations of the newly-appointed headteacher by the teachers, non-teaching staff, pupils and the governing body — and the external groups — parents, the local community, the wider community — are that the person would immediately behave in a 'headteacherly' manner and instantly be the professional leading the school. Each person having a pre-determined and individual view of what that behaviour looks like, the headteacher would be so judged as to her/his effectiveness.

The role of the LEA

The delegation of local authority expenditure to schools following the Education Reform Act (1988) has seen a considerable reduction in the number of LEA advisers or inspectors. Many of those persons, as representatives of the employing body (but also as fellow professionals who may, particularly in the primary sector have had experience of headship) would regularly spend time in schools with newly-appointed headteachers to maintain current knowledge of the developments in the school and also be a listening ear. Further, as an 'outsider', the friendly, neighbourhood pastoral adviser could be a testing ground for the ideas and initial thoughts of the newly-appointed head. The adviser would also have knowledge of some of the prior history of the school and could, therefore, indicate where areas of quicksand (fatal for those who do not know the terrain) might be found. The LEA adviser would also be aware of the local political situation, both internal and external to the school as well as informing the newly-appointed head of the interpretation of the LEA's curricular and other school-related policies. The reduction in a LEA pastoral advisory service will logically lead to an increased sense of isolation for all headteachers not just those recently appointed.

Does the employer not have a responsibility to ensure that the very expensive resource that has just been acquired reaches maximum effectiveness in the minimum possible time? If the answer to that question is in the affirmative then, to establish a mechanism by which such can be achieved in humane conditions and considerations would seem to be a very sensible and cost-efficient action.

Cluster support

Where a headteacher is appointed to the school in which she/he is a deputy or to a post in the same LEA where she/he may have developed as a deputy or in another leadership role, it is possible that there exist a set of persons — a professional network — in which may be found a single individual or small group with whom she/he feels affinity and in whom trust can be confidently placed.

Research findings (Bayliss S The Junior School Report, 1986) that headteachers become most effective between the third and seventh year of tenure is unsurprising since any new headteacher needs a period of discovery, meditation, concentration, before planning and execution of plans. What this leaves one with is a period during which the incumbent is less than effective. Obviously, much depends upon the criteria set against which effectiveness is measured, but if one is considering value for money and remember that the headteacher is, outside of plant costs, the most expensive part of the budget, then reducing the time during which the postholder is less than effective must be to the advantage of any institution.

How can the newly-appointed headteacher come to a state of effectiveness quickly? One answer is to ensure that the headteacher has access to a mentor. One solution might be to seek the assistance of the professional associations.

The role of the professional associations

There are a number of professional associations to which a head-teacher can gain membership. Those most concerned with head-teachers are the National Association of Headteachers (NAHT) and the Secondary Heads Association (SHA). Both organisations also accept deputy headteachers as members. Headteachers and deputies may also, but not additionally, be members of the National Union of Teachers (NUT) with its own section dealing with headteacher members, the National Association of Schoolmasters and Union of Women Teachers (NAS/UWT), again with a headteacher section, the Professional Association of Teachers (PAT) or no union at all.

That there is no single representative body for all teachers is perhaps a reason why such professionally developmental systems as mentoring do not exist as an entitlement throughout one's career. In *The Professional Development of School Administrators* (Allyn and Bacon 1992), Daresh J C and Playko M A see '*mentoring* as a way in which newcomers to professional education roles are made ready for their responsibilities' (p.109).

However, SHA here in Britain has established a centre for the development of current and aspiring headteacher and deputy head-teachers — the National Education Assessment Centre (NEAC). There has been some borrowing from across the Atlantic and particularly from the National Association of Secondary School Principals (NASSP) in policy and practice with regard to principal-ship. One of the elements of the centre's work is to determine strengths and areas for development of heads and aspiring heads and further to appoint a mentor to support the growth and development of the individual.

Daresh and Playko (1992) point out (p.115) that 'awareness that mentoring is an important concept that has implications for the ways in which beginning and aspiring administrators might enjoy more successful transitions from the world of teaching to the world of administering' (the term 'administrator' is the same as 'headteacher' in England).

Selecting a headteacher mentor

Mentors for headteacher should be other more experienced head-teachers, preferably working in the same LEA and operating in the same phase (that is, a mentor for a newly-appointed head in a secondary school should be mentored by someone holding an equivalent post in the same LEA).

Why is this aspect being highlighted? Some current practice (NEAC, CEMP) has crossed LEA boundaries in the search for mentors and, while there may be good reasons for doing that, some of the issues that arise as 'problems' for new heads will be concerned with the operational mechanism prevalent in the LEA in which she/he is employed. It is most likely that another headteacher in that LEA will know to whom the new head needs to address issues rather than merely the role. However, increasing local management of schools may reduce the need for interaction with the LEA and thus principles rather than practice may emerge as most significant in the longer term and thus cross-LEA mentoring may be singularly appropriate.

Headteacher skills to be attained and developed

According to the National Association of Secondary School Princi-pals (NASSP) centre model, sixteen skill areas have been identified to serve as the basis of a composite vision of principalship (Daresh and Playko 1992 pp. 70–72 *The professional development of school administrators*). The identified skill areas are as follows:

1. **Problem analysis:** The ability to seek out relevant data and analyse complex information to determine the important elements of a problem situation; searching for information for a purpose.
2. **Judgement:** The ability to reach logical conclusions and make high-quality decisions based on available information; skill in identifying educational needs and setting priorities; the ability to evaluate communications critically.
3. **Organizational ability:** The ability to plan, schedule, and control the work of others; skill in using resources in an optimal fashion; the ability to deal with a volume of paperwork and heavy demands on one's time.
4. **Leadership:** The ability to get others involved in solving problems; the ability to recognize when a group requires direction and to interact effectively with a group in order to guide them in accomplishing a task.
5. **Sensitivity:** The ability to perceive the needs, concerns, and personal problems of others; tact in dealing with persons from different backgrounds; the ability to deal effectively with people concerning emotional issues; knowledge of what information to communicate and to whom.
6. **Decisiveness:** The ability to recognize when a decision is required (disregarding the quality of the decision) and to act quickly.
7. **Range of interests:** Competence in discussing a variety of subjects — education, politics, current events, economics, and the like; active participation in events.
8. **Personal motivation:** The need to achieve in all activities; evidence that work is important to one's personal satisfaction; the ability to be self-policing.
9. **Educational values:** Possession of a well-reasoned educational philosophy.
10. **Stress tolerance:** The ability to perform under pressure and despite opposition; the ability to think on one's feet.
11. **Oral communication:** The ability to make clear oral presentations of facts and ideas.
12. **Written communication:** The ability to express ideas clearly in writing and to write appropriately for different audiences — students, parents, and others.
13. **Conflict management:** The willingness to intervene in conflict situations and the ability to develop solutions that are agreeable to all persons involved.

14. *Political astuteness:* The ability to perceive critical features of the environment, such as power structure, principal players, and special interest groups, and to formulate alternatives that reflect realistic expectations.
15. *Risk taking:* The extent to which calculated risks are taken on the basis of sound judgments.
16. *Creativity:* The ability to generate ideas that provide new and different solutions to management problems or opportunities.

These compare with the factors assessed as part of the competency-based assessment of heads and aspiring heads in the work of the National Educational Assessment Centre (Oliver 1993) shown below.

Administrative competencies

1. *Problem analysis:* Ability to seek out relevant data and analyze information to determine the important elements of a problem situation; searching for information with a purpose.
2. *Judgement:* Ability to reach logical conclusions and make high quality decisions based on available information; skill in identifying educational needs and setting priorities; ability to evaluate critically written communications.
3. *Organisational ability:* Ability to plan, schedule and control the work of others; skill in using resources in an optimal fashion; ability to deal with a volume of paperwork and heavy demands on one's time.
4. *Decisiveness:* Ability to recognise when a decision is required (disregarding the quality of the decision) and to act quickly.

Interpersonal competencies

5. *Leadership:* Ability to get others involved in solving problems; ability to recognise when a group requires direction, to interact with a group effectively and to guide them to the accomplishment of a task.
6. *Sensitivity:* Ability to perceive the needs, concerns and problems of others; skill in resolving conflicts; tact in dealing with persons from different backgrounds; ability to deal effectively with people concerning emotional issues; knowing what information to communicate and to whom.
7. *Stress tolerance:* Ability to perform under pressure and during opposition; ability to think on one's feet.

Communicative competencies

8. *Oral communication:*   Ability to make clear oral presentation of facts or ideas.
9. *Written:*   Ability to express clearly in writing; to communication: write appropriately for different audiences — students, teachers, parents et al.

Personal breadth competencies

10. *Range of interests:*   Ability to discuss a variety of subjects — educational, political, current events, economic etc.; desire to actively participate in events.
11. *Personal:*   Need to achieve in all activities attempted; motivation: evidence that work is important to personal satisfaction; ability to be self-evaluating.
12. *Educational values:*   Possession of a well reasoned educational philosophy; receptiveness to new ideas and change.

An abbreviated table of management attributes comparing NASSP, NEAC, the Cheshire Education Management Development Programme (CEMP) and the more general Management Charter Initiative (MCI) models is shown in Figure 7.1.

Figure 7.1 indicates areas of need for the role of headteacher and thus aspects for development which might form the starting point for mentoring. Indeed, the NASSP and NEAC give an assessment on these attributes.

It is interesting to note that absent from the NASSP derived competencies which the NEAC have compiled is 'political astuteness'. One questions such an omission and suggests that such positive action by the NEAC is, in fact, a 'political' act.

Forms of support

Shapiro, Haseltine and Rowe (1978) suggested that there is a continuum of advisory relationships . . .

'Peer pal':   Someone at the same level as yourself, with whom you share information, strategies and mutual support for mutual benefit
Guide: Someone who can explain the system but is usually not in a position to champion a protege
Sponsor: Someone less powerful than a patron in promoting and shaping the career of a protege

NASSP	CEMP	MCI	NEAC
Creativity	Vision	Initiative	
Organizational ability	Planning skill	Organizational ability	Organizational ability
Problem analysis	Critical thinking	Problem analysis	Problem analysis
Leadership	Leadership skill	Leadership skills	Leadership
Decisiveness	Persistence	Decisiveness	Decisiveness
Political astuteness	Influence skills	Influence skills	
Conflict management	Interpersonal relationships	Conflict management	
Risk-taking	Self-confidence	Maintenance & future orientation	
Personal motivation	Capacity for development of self and others	Develop self and others	Personal motivation
Sensitivity	Empathy	Counselling	Sensitivity
Stress tolerance	Stress tolerance		Stress tolerance
Educational values		Company values	Educational values
Oral communication		Oral communication	Oral communication
Written communication		Written communication	Written communication
Judgement		Judgement	Judgement
Range of interests			Range of interests
		Recruitment	
		Monitoring	
		Evaluation skills	

Figure 7.1

Patron: An influential person who uses his or her own power to help a protegee advance in his or her career
Mentor: An intensive paternalistic relationship in which an individual assumes the role of both teacher and advocate (Daresh and Playko 1992)

Some of the above suggestions are replicated by and added to by School Management South who list the following roles for mentors of headteachers: coach, confidante, counsellor, facilitator, guide, listener, networker, protector, role-model, sounding board, sponsor, trainer, tutor.

For headteachers, the notion of 'peer pal' is probably the most appropriate and is exemplified by the interaction of headteachers in clusters, pyramids and in their professional association activities. In the course of headteacher intercourse, the roles suggested by School Management South could be recognised. Through such intercourse, lifelong relationships can be formed.

One factor which must be realised in relation to the mentoring of headteachers by other headteachers and/or LEA staff is the uniqueness of the situation in which each headteacher finds her/himself.

It is patently obvious that a particular solution to one particular issue in one particular school when applied to another when a similar situation arises can be disastrous. Although the stage setting may be identical, the players are different. Thus, a comedy may be turned into a tragedy.

The traps for mentors are seen by School Management South as: being judgmental, being over-protective, being a surrogate manager, attempting psychotherapy, and encouraging passive dependency. Omniscience is sometimes a drawback to effective mentoring.

Daresh and Playko (1992, p.112) warn of the danger that '. . . mentoring can be potentially harmful to growth if and when proteges' [mentees] 'develop too great a reliance on mentors, who are expected to provide all possible answers to all possible questions.'

Resourcing

Resourcing the practice of mentoring of beginning headteachers will be a key factor in determining success. Like any other decision regarding individual and institutional development there are likely to be cost implications.

Governing bodies may question the 'value for money' in buying in additional aid for someone who in the eye of those appointing is the most capable professional in their institution and who is to lead their school, perhaps in competition with a neighbouring school from which their head may be given support by the head of that rival school.

Who chooses the mentor?

One would expect that in the case of headteachers — far more than other new teachers — the individual would, from the interaction with other headteachers from their locale or branch of a professional association, find an individual (or set of individuals) in whom she/he feels personal and professional confidence. Very often, particularly in urban areas, there are informal and well-established and cluster or pyramid meetings of headteachers who act as a self-support group for one another. The sum of collective headteachers' knowledge and nous is generally sufficient to enable any individual headteacher — newly-appointed or otherwise — to gain new insights into challenges which face her/him. As Daresh and Playko (1992) remind us: ' "New" administrators are not new to schools . . . beginning, principals have often had experience as lead teachers or in other leadership roles.' One of the reasons that they are appointed as headteachers is because of the greater skills and knowledge they have developed.

A further advantage of meeting with other headteachers who work in close proximity is that a more dynamic set of options becomes available and there is additionally a reduction in the sense of isolation — being the only one who faces that problem and with no-one to give assistance. (Headteachers do not always make the best use of their deputies or other senior teachers in problem-solving. Sometimes the deputies or other senior teachers may be the problem.)

Stress tolerance may be a headteacher competence (see above) but any means by which stress can be reduced must surely be advantageous and cluster or pyramid meetings are less hazardous to health than alcohol or drug abuse. They are also less costly to schools' budgets in the longer term since absence of a headteacher through stress-related illness increases the strain throughout the school and may well lead to a loss in the school's leadership, direction and consequent fall in pupil numbers.

Whether there is a mentoring system established for all newly-appointed headteachers or not, newly-appointed headteachers will still make the occasional gaffe but, if there is mentoring and it is taken seriously, the size of the blunder is likely to be reduced and thus mentoring will have paid for itself.

In practice, most mentoring is not costed as an item of expenditure. It takes place in an undirected and person-centred way with compacts — unwritten contracts — between two or more consenting professionals. How these relationships develop is more to do with the needs of those individuals involved. It must not be regarded as parasitic: the newly-appointed headteacher taking the time and energy of the more experienced principal. There is gain for the mentor not least in the rewarding and regenerative mid-life task of 'generativity' — 'concern for and interest in guiding the next generation' (Merriam 1983).

Further gain for the mentor of headteachers is the renaissance of a more reflective approach to her/his own daily work. As one experienced headteacher remarked,

> When listening to the approach to staff involvement in decision-making adopted by one of my younger headteacher colleagues, I began to reconsider my own approach and its appropriateness in the brave, new, post-ERA world. As headteacher, I had always believed that it was my responsibility to make the decisions. Perhaps, it was time to change.

Yet another was rekindled by the animated behaviour and excitement shown by her mentee in actually gaining a new headship.

> I was mentally exhausted by the enthusiasm and energy she displayed and was reminded of my own early feelings. I thought to myself 'Why don't I still feel like that?' I determined that from that day I would be less cynical and present a more positive face about the changes in front of us. And I have! But it hasn't been easy!

Like all leaders, headteachers need to have a secure environment where they can explore ideas for maintenance and change with people who understand the role, the environment and the time in which they are living. One possible model worthy of further exploration is that of a Revansian Action Learning Set (Revans 1980), where managers from different organisations meet regularly to give one another support in the form of questioning their premises, acting as devil's advocates, sharing ideas and strategies, dealing with real problems in real time, yet remaining non-judgmental. Such a model avoids dependency on one mentor and allows the shared wisdom to be available to all and not just the inexperienced.

If we are to learn and develop as managers, as headteachers, then we shall only do so at our own pace and through our own experience (albeit supplemented by the divined experience of others). However, it must be remembered that one does not have to have put one's own hand into the flame to 'know' that one will get burned in a fire.

Characteristics of school administration which separate it from teaching

There are, as Daresh and Playko (1992, p.84) identify, 'several fundamental differences between the roles of teacher and administrator (headteacher).' So to apply the same mentoring approach would be inappropriate even though generic skills such as listening and other interpersonal skills would still apply.

They (ibid., pp.84–85) identify some 'characteristics of school administration that make it quite unlikely that any specific activities designed to improve the quality of preservice preparation will have a similar value for another group of professional educators.'

1. There is insufficient research on administration. The question 'What do effective principals do?' is not yet clearly answered in the same way as what constitutes effective teacher behaviour

    Principals, they suggest (ibid. p.85), 'should spend more time observing teachers in their classes — less time on the public address system.'

2. 'New' administrators are not new to schools

    'In most states there is an expectation that administrative personnel will have spent from three to five years in a classroom before receiving an initial certificate . . . every person moving from the classroom to an administrative position at least knows what a school looks like, how students tend to behave, and what parents are likely to ask or demand. (Daresh and Playko 1992)

    It is most likely in the UK that most of those attaining headship have had considerably more than five years as a teacher. Yet they are unlikely to have received any formal training for headship.

3. Administrators are formal leaders.

    On becoming a headteacher ('administrator') then automatically assumes the formal authority, power and control of a school. The headteacher is responsible for 'the day-to-day management of the school.' (School Teachers Pay and Conditions, DFE)

4. Administrative 'peers' usually are not equal to the beginner.

    There is no easy route for someone who has just become a headteacher to gain experience through working with someone else with similar responsibilities to resolve issues facing her/him. Once again the uniqueness of the individual and her/his school act against the use of former practice

A key recommendation in terms of the development of head-teachers has to be a more meritocratic approach with the opportunities to gain 'the knowledge' needed for headship. If the attributes or skills are agreed and clearly identified, then the role of the mentor would have greater definition; the target areas would be clearer.

Pre-service programs are effective only when they promote the understanding that seeking support and guidance from others in the organization is an action that ultimately promotes strength, not weakness.

As one beginning headteacher said of his mentor, 'Coming from outside the LEA, I found it a real advantage having been put in touch with an experienced head who knew the ins and outs of the authority. Knowing that she was there, just a phone call away was a great comfort to me. I didn't have to display my ignorance to the representatives — the advisers — or the LEA.'

'I had always regarded my mentor — a long-standing and well-known headteacher in the district — with almost awe and certainly distant respect and was pleasantly surprised to come to know him as a friend as well as a supportive colleague. It also gave me hope when he admitted that sometimes he did not know the answers.'

'At first, it was my *cris de coeur* to which my mentor would patiently listen. Although, initially, she suggested many alternatives which were available for my consideration, very soon, the response, "Well, what do you think you should do?" became the norm. After a while, I began to realise that the "problems" were *my* "problems" and the "solutions" I had to own.'

'Although the mentor to whom I was allotted was a pleasant and helpful person, our educational philosophies and approaches to the staff were quite different, which was apparent from an early stage in our meetings. Before long we drifted apart and except for occasional headteacher meetings called by the professional association, I rarely see him. I now tend to test out my thoughts and ideas with heads whom I have found to have similar views to my own. . . . On reflection, I suppose that I could have gained greatly from someone who caused me to think and defend my opinions and actions, but the situation is, perhaps, irredeemable for me and my named mentor.'

Recommendations for future development

As moves towards a more formal competence-based approach to teaching become firmer, it is increasingly likely that the role of the headteacher and principal development will be similarly focused. Since mentoring is about developing professionalism and not merely technical prowess, an entitlement to the services of a headteacher mentor who is both proficient as a headteacher and committed to the principle of generativity should be available to beginning head-teachers.

There should, too, be consideration given to induction as an obligation upon the employer — in most cases this would still be the LEA — to provide such for any headteacher new to the employing body as a headteacher. This provision would be equally available as a right to experienced headteachers new to that authority. The inductor may or may not eventually be one and the same person as the mentor.

Newly-appointed headteachers, it must be recognised, are diffe-rent from other newly-appointed staff. They are usually very experienced and skilled teachers whose new role separates them from other teachers. While the newly-appointed headteacher will certainly gain from the knowledge and skills and wisdom of other senior staff (and, indeed, the whole staff) of the school, she/he will also gain from (and contribute to) the collective wisdom of a group of fellow headteachers. While a particular headteacher might be assigned by the LEA (or NEAC or a professional association) as mentor to a newly-appointed head, how the relationship develops and its usefulness to the mentee will depend not only upon the skills and abilities of that mentor but also upon the way the two interact. The issues relating to matching are at least as critical here as for a newly-qualified teacher. Philosophies and personalities will make a marked difference.

It may be advantageous to the mentee for there to be a number of fellow heads on whom she/he can call. With this system, the mentee can build up relationships with several before finally coming to a symbiotic relationship with one or two. One means to such an end is the development of cluster groups.

Another would be for an LEA to bring together newly-appointed heads together with more experienced and empathetic heads to work together during one or two INSET days. (Some LEAs have main-tained a proportion of the Professional Development days for their priorities. Is there a greater priority than seeking to ensure the rapid effectiveness of one's employees?) From such, can an array of potential mentors be experienced by the mentee and a reflective preference declared.

Looking for mentors for headteachers

In the work of Daresh and Playko (1990 and 1992) a number of characteristics of mentors is presented to aid selection.

1. Mentors should have experience as practising school administrators, and they should be generally regarded by their peers and others as being effective
2. Mentors must demonstrate generally accepted positive leadership qualities, such as (but not necessarily limited to):
    (a) Good oral and written communication skills
    (b) Intelligence
    (c) Past, present and future understanding with simultaneous orientation
    (d) Acceptance of multiple alternative solutions to complex problems
    (e) Clarity of vision and the ability to share that vision with others in the organisation
    (f) Well-developed interpersonal skills and sensitivities
3. Mentors need to be able to ask just the right questions of beginning administrators . . .
4. Mentors must accept 'another way of doing things' . . .
5. Mentors should express the desire to see people go beyond their present levels of performance (even if it means the apprentice outstripping the master)
6. Mentors need to model the principle of continuous learning and reflection
7. Mentors must exhibit an awareness of the political and social realities of life in at least one school system (for 'system' read 'LEA')

Additionally they (ibid) include Haensly's and Edlind's (1986) 'ideal' mentor characteristics:

1. Outstanding knowledge, skills and expertise in a particular domain
2. Enthusiasm that is sincere, convincing, and, most important, constantly conveyed to their proteges
3. The ability to communicate a clear picture of their personal attitudes, values and ethical standards
4. The ability to communicate sensitively the type of feedback that is needed regarding the protege's development and progress toward desirable standards of competence and professional behaviour
5. The ability to listen sensitively to their protege's ideas, doubts, concerns, and enthusiastic outpourings
6. A caring attitude and a belief in their protege's potential
7. Flexibility and a sense of humour
8. A restrained sense of guidance so that proteges may develop as independently as possible

There are many experienced headteachers who have the above virtues (though many are too modest to admit to such and some may be latent characteristics). Additional skill enhancement training for those who would wish to develop themselves as mentors is available.

If the role of headteacher (which commences on the first day of appointment — and sometimes before one's former contract has ended) is to reach maximum possible effectiveness in the minimum possible time and simultaneously reduce the anxiety that comes from the isolation of the post, then headteacher mentoring becomes an unquestionably cost-effective activity.

8 Mentoring and management development

John West-Burnham

Introduction

The purpose of this chapter is to explore the relationship between the concept of effective management development and the culture and techniques of mentoring. The chapter develops a definition of management development, identifies the relationship between this definition and mentoring and then proposes a number of strategies to support management development using mentoring techniques.

The nature and purpose of management development in schools

Everard (1986) identifies the key function of management development as 'an approach that supports, promotes and is harmoniously related to the development of the organisation'. The emphasis is on linking individual performance to organisational improvement. The purpose of management development is therefore to provide opportunities for individuals to enhance their skills, knowledge and experience so as to allow them to contribute more effectively to the achievement of organisational goals. This raises fundamental issues about the clarity of organisational goals and the extent to which individual roles and responsibilities reflect these outcomes.

Historically in schools there has been a temptation to see management development as being the responsibility of the individual and largely motivated by career development, the impact of this is reflected in the comments in the 1993 Report of the Pay Review Board. They identified a number of 'management weaknesses' e.g.

- A failure to focus sufficiently on pupils' achievements, on outcomes as well as processes
- Ineffective implementation of agreed policies . . . some schools painstakingly establish such policies but then put little effort into their delivery
- Middle managements . . . which do not recognise or exercise their managerial role, or which are not used in that way by heads
- Confusion between administration and management, with undue emphasis [on] . . . the former. . . . (pp.38–39)

The message here is one of the failure of management development to be integrated into practice, of training not informing behaviour and role perceptions not being defined or changed.

One explanation of the origin of these concerns is the apparent dichotomy between training and development and the job itself. All too often training and development are not integrated into practice; the School Management Task Force (1990) identified the 'current emphasis' in training provision as 'tutor-directed courses, off-site training, predetermined times, oral presentations, a provider determined syllabus and an emphasis on knowledge acquisition' (p.21). In essence management development was about attending short or award-bearing courses with insufficient emphasis on individual performance enhancement, application to the actual job or correlation with the school's goals.

Margerison (1991) challenges this approach (which is by no means unique to the education service):

Management development is a way of doing business. It is an integral part of management. Management development is real work. It is not a preparation for work. It is not a substitute for work. It is the real thing if properly organised. (p.3)

This approach requires a fundamental cultural shift, doing the job is the developmental activity not the acquisition of skills or knowledge. They are an important contribution to the possibility of improvement but the fundamental criterion has to be the extent to which management behaviour actually changes. If there is no integration of training with the job then the training only has value as a preparation for 'Mastermind' and is about as developmental as 'bungee jumping'.

A further inhibition upon effective management development is the perception of the concept of 'management' — it is too often perceived as a noun rather than a verb. Shipman (1990) provides a powerful caution:

> The headteacher will not be able to cope . . . . Delegation becomes essential, yet insufficient. Being at the centre can still mean being overwhelmed. The only solution will be to empower staff to take decisions. Management has to involve the spread of leadership, not just delegation. (p.22)

It is an irony that in education the notion of management has become inextricably associated with status, hierarchy and gender imbalances. Becoming a 'manager' is associated with upward movement through the complex state of the salary structure. Yet if any new entrant to teaching had chosen to enter another employment sector they would have been a 'manager' from the outset. Management development in schools that does not recognise, reinforce, celebrate and integrate effective classroom practice is denying a powerful set of common experiences and reinforcing the artificial divide between being 'a teacher' and being 'a manager'. The problem is one of establishing a genuine dialogue between the principles of managing children's learning and those of managing adult learning. Models of what it means to manage and what it means to learn have high degrees of compatibility.

Equally the relationship between teacher and learner can be replicated as that between teacher and manager. The model in Figure 8.1 was developed by students at Mt Edgecumbe High School in Alaska USA and it makes the telling point that effective learning and effective managing are not parallel activities — they are the same activity.

The way in which teachers' learning is managed provides a powerful model in the school for the way in which teachers manage student learning.

The problematics of the artificial divide are well illustrated by Joyce and Showers (1980). Their analysis of the effectiveness of staff development in education established a clear correlation between access to the full portfolio of learning activities and the extent to which principle is actually translated into habitual practice.

Joyce and Showers defined four potential levels of impact of training which may be summarised as (1) awareness, (2) understanding, (3) application, (4) integration and transfer. They also identified five of the most commonly used training methods, (1) presentation, (2) modelling, (3) practising, (4) feedback, (5) coaching. The crucial conclusion of the research was that full integration of new knowledge or skills was only achieved when all five training methods were used. This would seem to reinforce the concerns expressed above that training which is externally managed and has agendas which do not

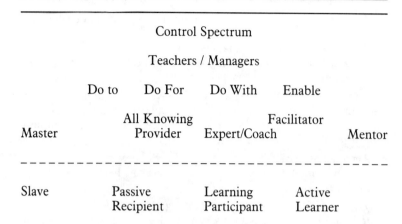

The way in which teachers' learning is managed provides a powerful model in the school for the way in which teachers manage student learning.

Figure 8.1   Linking learning and managing

grow out of the individual's job and is not supported in the workplace, will not work.

Joyce and Showers' work does not deny the validity or relevance of knowledge based training but stresses its limited potential:

> If any of [the] components are left out, the impact of training will be weakened in the sense that fewer numbers of people will progress to the transfer level (which is the only level that has significant meaning for school improvement). (p.384)

This view reinforces Margerison's definition above that development occurs in doing the actual job supported by reflection and feedback and coaching. This immediately raises the question: who provides the feedback and coaching? Who develops the developers? This in turn raises the issue of the purpose and role of managers in schools.

A number of indicators demonstrate the potential difficulty of managers in schools as developers:

1. The lack of any reference in a school's aims or mission statement to adult learning

2.   The absence of requirements in job descriptions to develop self
     and colleagues
3.   The limited systems available for needs analysis
4.   The limited use of training opportunities and the failure to
     integrate them into everyday practice

Torrington and Weightman (1989) have drawn attention to the
problem of role perception in two ways: the concept of agendas and
networks and the distinction between leadership, management and
administration. They argue that

> Agendas are lists of things to be done. Networks . . . are co-
> operative relationships with people who can help to get things
> done. (p.112)

The empirical research that Torrington and Weightman con-
ducted raised serious questions about the use of management time in
secondary schools. They found (1989, p.102) that their sample of 33
secondary deputy heads spent an average of 31 per cent of their time
on administrative tasks, with a range of 12–77 per cent. They had
suggested a definition of administrative work as 'that which could be
done by an intelligent 16 year old'. The implications are clear; if
administrative time is combined with a classroom commitment then
the time available for managing is compromised and this says
nothing about the quality of that management. The opportunity cost
of managers working on low-level agendas is an impoverished
network and a very limited capacity to manage and lead.

However to change this pattern of behaviour requires a fundamental attitudinal shift which will in turn allow effective management behaviour. Three concepts are helpful in defining a culture in
which genuine management development is possible — the learning
organisation, continuous development and continuous improvement.

Handy (1989) following Drucker (1989) argues that we live in a
time of 'discontinuous change' (most schools in England and Wales
will readily identify with this concept) and that to respond to this
situation we have to learn faster than the rate of change. According
to Handy's model this learning has to be, in effect, institutionalised
i.e.

1.   There have to be formal, organisation wide opportunities for
     review, questioning and reflection
2.   The organisation's values, mission and future are at the centre of
     all activity
3.   There is a constant process of re-framing the organisation in its
     environment
4.   There is 'negative capability', it is able to assimilate failure and
     mistakes as learning opportunities

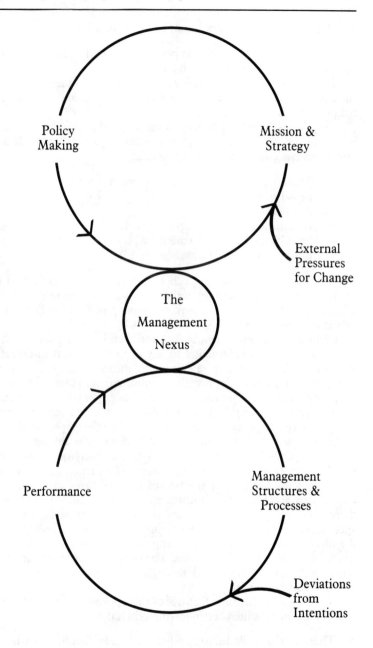

Figure 8.2   Management learning in the school
(after Garratt 1987 p. 79)

4.   There is an overt commitment to caring and learning

Using these components it is possible to modify Garratt's (1987) model of the learning organisation.

The important feature of this model is that it sets management in the role of mediating between demands for change and organisational procedures and processes.

The means by which managers carry out this mediating role is best encapsulated in the concept of continuous development. Wood (1988) defines continuous development as

—   The integration of learning with work
—   Self-directed learning
—   A process, not a technique
—   An attitude, a way of tackling work
—   Simultaneous improvement in the performance of employees and organisations (pp.9–13)

This view has very strong echoes of Margerison's definition of management development quoted above and serves to reinforce the argument that effective management development is implicit, integrated and continuous.

Continuous improvement is the central concept of Total Quality Management, it is fundamental to any of the numerous interpretations of TQM. In essence it rejects pragmatic expediency and 'short-termism' and replaces them with a central commitment to the long term improvement of products and services supplied to customers. In the context of TQM customers are internal and external, employees as well as purchasers or end-users. The development of staff is therefore as subject to continuous improvement as any product.

The Japanese concept is that of Kaizen: planning to improve step-by-step, through incremental stages. The gardening enthusiast never 'finishes' her garden apart from seasonal tasks there are new plants, new arrangements, features etc. to be considered. Although there may be a long-term vision, it has to be achieved through specific, concrete and practical activities. So it is with development; the ideal is only achieved by focusing on the specifics, the elephant has to be eaten in bite-size chunks. The management of learning in a school will only be improved through the enhancement of actual management behaviour.

A summary of the main features of this approach identified so far in this chapter produces the following criteria:

•   There is a clear definition and shared understanding of what it means to be a manager and of the components of effective managing

- Central to the management task is managing the performance of colleagues through empowerment rather than control
- Performance is managed through enhancing the capacity to do the actual job
- Enhanced capacity is the result of applying knowledge and skills in real situations and getting feedback which leads to planning
- There is always a better way and the process is therefore continuous

Mentoring as a strategy for management development

If the model of management development outlined above is accepted then its potential links with mentoring readily emerge. The definitions provided in chapter 1 provide clear parallels. The argument in chapter 6 for the link between mentoring and appraisal indicates a high degree of correlation. However it is worth reinforcing some of the key components of effective integration.

Firstly a school needs an explicit policy for management development which makes reference to:

1. The key purpose and values of management development related to children's learning
2. The entitlement of all staff to support and development in their management roles
3. The responsibility of all managers to develop colleagues
4. The use of appraisal as the process of needs-analysis
5. The responsibility of individuals to engage in developmental activities
6. The resources that are available to support management development

Such a policy should be an exemplification of a component of the school's mission statement relating to the adults in the school community and the specific priorities should be expressed in the annual development plan and INSET programme. Without this degree of formalisation and institutionalisation management development may be perceived as marginal and its delivery will be ad-hoc and random.

This process of formalisation can be extended by the inclusion of appropriate statements in the job descriptions of management post holders, e.g:

To be appraised and to appraise staff in accordance with the School's Professional Development Strategy and to engage in

INSET activities so as to enhance personal and professional effectiveness and career development in the context of the School's Mission and Development Plan.

These approaches argue for a model of mentoring that is formalised, structured and long term. This is not to diminish the validity of mentoring relationships that are informal and short-term but to reinforce the notion that one of the most effective ways of managing staff is to mentor. Shea (1992, p. 14) has produced a helpful model (see Figure 8.3) to analyse the possible types of relationship and this has been modified to describe situations in schools.

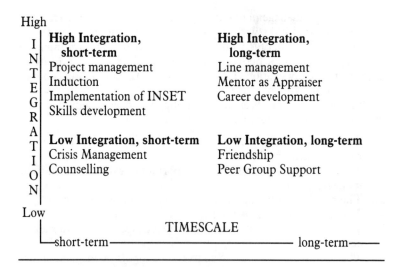

Figure 8.3   Mentoring relationships

In the context of this chapter it is argued that the integrated, long-term relationship is the norm for management development. However integrated, short term relationships will be appropriate for induction, preparation for a career change or to deal with a specific initiative. Informal relationships occur naturally in any healthy organisation and wise managers will leave them to flourish. They can provide an important source of support and guidance outside the formal structures and processes. For example a newly qualified teacher may be 'taken under the wing' of an experienced teacher, a new appraiser may seek advice and counselling from a colleague. These are powerful relationships and can only enhance effectiveness

However they do not replace the formal and structural responsibilities. However just because a relationship is formal in structural terms this does not mean it has to be formal or constrained in interpersonal terms (see chapter 4). It is equally important to stress that the mentoring relationship has the potential to be mutually beneficial i.e. 'In explaining to you I increase my understanding', 'In coaching another I improve my own performance'.

The use of mentoring in a formal and integrated way does raise the issue of the definition of satisfactory performance. There is a need for definitions of performance to act as a 'benchmark', a reference point to allow the review of current performance and the identification of appropriate strategies to achieve a required standard. Without such definitions management development may well be valid in personal terms but may not be relevant to organisational needs. Mentors and their clients therefore need to work within a context of agreed definitions and specifications. The source of such benchmarks might include:

1. School policies, development plans, schemes of work, job descriptions, staff handbook, etc
2. The OFSTED *Framework for Inspection*
3. Criteria for appraisal (see West-Burnham 1993)
4. Agreed competences for education management (see Earley 1992)
5. The competences defined by the Management Charter Initiative (see The School Management Handbook, 1992)

Which of these are used, and how they are applied and defined is very much a matter for the school but effective school management does presuppose consistency of purpose and delivery and the most basic notion of equity demands common standards and outcomes in the management of INSET.

Mentoring activities for management development

This section describes, with examples, the sorts of way in which mentors can work with their clients in the context of management development. none of them is unique to the mentor–client relationships but they have the particular characteristics that

1. The activity grows out of and is applied to the client's job.
2. The long term nature of the relationship facilitates modification and review
3. The management relationship helps to ensure that something happens and is directly evaluated

One of the important attributes of using mentoring as the vehicle for these activities is the increased confidence that action and improvement will result.

Knowledge

In the context of management development there is little space for knowledge for its own sake. Managers have limited time available to find out what they need to know and then to find the relevant information. At the same time knowledge in the sense of theoretical models, examples of practice and analysis and interpretation is a fundamental component of management understanding.

The role of the mentor is to:

— Clarify what information is actually required
— Provide it if possible
— Suggest sources and facilitate access to them
— Provide follow-up by way of interpretation, reflection, application or further investigation

There are a vast number of potential activities in this area, from passing on a newspaper clipping describing good practice to taking a masters degree in education management. This book itself could be used in this way but so could access to a colleague or attendance at a short course. In all cases the role of the mentor is to help diagnose the need, access the resource and help translate theory into practice.

Skills

This is an area where the mentor–client relationship has the greatest potential for improving management practice. Again the role of the mentor is threefold, diagnosing, resourcing and applying. It is in the resourcing stage that the relationship is most fruitful as the way in which mentor and client work together can be a direct exemplar of many management skills. The possibility of artificiality is lessened because the learning takes place within a genuine management relationship.

An appropriate example is that of appraisal skills; because the mentor is already the client's appraiser there is a genuine management relationship and an opportunity to apply the skills. The difference that mentoring brings to appraisal is that the appraiser/mentor uses the process as a learning vehicle by

— Consciously providing a role-model
— Explaining what is happening at each stage

—   Building in opportunities for shared reflection based on feed-
    back
—   Incorporating references to shared training
—   Being available for reflection when the appraisee has become an
    appraiser

In this way training and practice are integrated and the process is
mutually beneficial. This same approach can be applied to time
management, communication skills, team building etc. It is a good
example of the Joyce and Showers model at work.

Networking

One of the strongest arguments for the mentor to be the line
manager or team leader is that she/he will often be 'older and wiser'
(not necessarily in chronological or qualification terms). Reference
has already been made to Torrington and Weightman's view that
effective managers have sophisticated networks. A crucial role of the
mentor is to facilitate the networking of the client. All organisations
operate on the basis of formal and informal structures with the latter
often being the more significant, especially in schools. The mentor
can provide support by:

—   Identifying appropriate networks
—   Helping to negotiate access
—   Supporting the outcomes of network activity

An important factor is the fact that mentor and client are
themselves the basis of a network and both can enhance their
partnership by extending it into a range of broader networks.
    Examples of networking possibilities include:

—   Women managers in a school
—   A 'cluster' of primary school headteachers
—   Heads of department with common appraisal targets
—   Deputy headteachers working to implement new initiatives

The advantages of such networks will include:

•   Pooling of collective wisdom and experience
•   Shared problem solving
•   'No risk' discussion of problems and 'failures'
•   Dissemination of good practice
•   Enrichment of the mentor–client relationship

Coaching

This is a complex activity for the mentor as it involves a balance of directing and facilitating without inhibiting the client's sense of ownership and commitment. The credibility of the mentor as practitioner is therefore all important. The components of effective coaching are:

— Setting clear performance expectations
— Agreeing realistic targets
— Identifying 'low risk' learning situations
— Providing relevant, objective feedback
— Building self-esteem and confidence
— Reinforcing success
— Ensuring repetition of appropriate behaviour

For example:

A newly appointed member of a senior management team confides to his mentor that he finds it very difficult to contribute to team meetings, his mentor, also a member of the team, helps him to analyse the problem and agrees a strategy. The possible causes are:

— Natural diffidence in a new situation
— Fear of speaking 'out of turn'
— Lack of knowledge
— Dominance of meetings by two members of the team
— Limited time to prepare

The following strategy is agreed:

— A meeting before SMT meetings to identify possible areas for the client to contribute
— The client to prepare possible contributions in advance
— The mentor to specifically involve her client
— A meeting after each SMT meeting to review progress and plan future strategy

This approach can also be applied to a range of other situations, e.g. the production of a departmental development plan, the management of a training day, developing a strategy to work with an underachieving colleague.

Reflection

This is perhaps the most important way in which a mentor can support a client, without reflection there is no learning. Schon (1983) refers to 'reflection in action' or a 'reflective conversation with the situation' (p. 42).

It is one of the functions of the mentor to stimulate this 'reflective conversation' and help generate the creativity, inventiveness and observation. At the most basic level it is a matter of 'two heads are better than one' or reflection presupposes a mirror. The relationship is characterised in Figure 8.4.

TASK

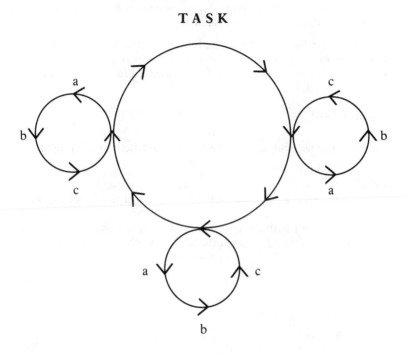

Figure 8.4   Mentoring and reflection

The manager is directly responsible for the task but at agreed intervals the mentor is involved to aid reflection at critical stages in the completion of the task. Each reflective stage is characterised by (a) sharing, (b) reviewing, (c) planning.

The role of the mentor is to support the reflective stages of the process by using a variety of techniques, e.g.

— Questioning to support analysis and drawing conclusions
— Listening to help the client describe behaviour
— Challenging assumptions and conclusions
— Proposing insights and explanations
— Giving feedback to test understanding
— Describing behaviour as a result of observation or data collection

This approach is appropriate in almost all mentoring situations but it may be particularly relevant in the following:

- Reviewing the management of a task or project
- Reflecting on the first term in a new post
- Preparing for an interview for a promotion by having a 'dress rehearsal' with the mentor as interviewer

Whatever the context it is the role of the mentor to support her/his client in a process of analysis which allows conclusions to be drawn by the client which will inform enhanced future performance.

Conclusion

This chapter has shown that effective management development:

— Grows out of the actual job
— Is a responsibility of managers and their managers
— Depends on a learning rather than control model of management
— Is consistent with the notion of line-management
— Can be facilitated through the use of mentoring techniques

Appendix 1

1.0 COMPETENCES FOR ITT PGCE Secondary (1993) — Manchester Metropolitan University, Crewe + Alsager Faculty

1.1 SUBJECT KNOWLEDGE

By the end of your course of initial training newly qualified teachers should be able to demonstrate:

1.1.1 an understanding of the knowledge, concepts and skills of their specialist subjects and of the place of these subjects in the school curriculum.

1.1.2 knowledge and understanding of the National Curriculum and attainment targets (NCATs) and the programmes of study (PoS) in the subjects they are preparing to teach, together with an understanding of the frame work of the statutory requirements.

Knowledge of Curriculum Content

- initial core subjects, own phase.
- then foundation subjects, own phase.
- core subjects, other phase.
- foundation subjects, other phase.
- all curriculum areas, both phases.

Subject knowledge is expressed in terms of

- programmes of study.
- levels of attainment.

- attainment targets.
- assessment issues in the subject area.

1.1.3   a breadth and depth of subject knowledge extending beyond PoS and examination syllabuses in school.
- knowledge of treatment of cross-curricular skills, themes and dimensions, as they apply to those parts of the National Curriculum which they are required to teach.
- awareness of professional associations, journals, etc. relating to their subject area.

1.2   SUBJECT APPLICATION
By the end of your course of initial training, newly qualified teachers should be able to:

1.2.1   Set appropriate aims and objectives;
- ability to recognise the main purpose(s) of a lesson or activity planned by another (e.g. class teacher).
- understanding of the terms, and of the difference between aims and objectives; to distinguish yet relate the terms. To state aims and objectives in terms of what children are to know, understand and/or be able to do.
- ability to set aims appropriate to the context, particularly pupils' learning needs.
- ability to set objectives appropriate to the contexts, particularly the needs of the group/class.

1.2.2   produce coherent lesson plans which take account of PoS, NCATs and of the school's curriculum policies;
- demonstrate awareness of equal opportunities in planning learning e.g. the issues and effects of racism and sexism in planning learning opportunities.

1.2.3   ensure continuity and progression within and between classes and in subjects;
- devise outline plans.
- demonstrate knowledge of the sequences required in pupils' learning (e.g. linear progression necessary in some aspects of maths).
- plan a series of lessons (block plan) where the subject matter develops logically, sequentially and pupils' needs are met.
- construct a lesson plan which includes references to aims, objectives, organisation, management and resource issues.
- contextualise lesson and block plans in terms of National Curriculum Programmes of Study and Attainment Targets and other relevant contexts.

- plan for longer periods of time (half-term or term) coherent and progressive sequences of work.

1.2.4 set appropriately demanding expectations for pupils;
- match and differentiate work according to the individual needs of pupils in a given context.
- demonstrate an understanding of the stages of intellectual and physical development.
- demonstrate an awareness of equal opportunities issues in teacher expectations.
- demonstrate an awareness of SEN including those of the more able.
- convey high expectations of all pupils.

1.2.5 employ a range of teaching strategies appropriate to the age, ability and attainment level of pupils;
- employ strategies appropriate to the individual needs of pupils in a given context.
- demonstrate an awareness of equal opportunities in teacher–pupil interactions.
- demonstrate skills in varying activities and emphasis.
- use appropriate pace, timing and pupil involvement.

1.2.6 present subject content in clear language and in a stimulating manner;
- use language to further pupils' understanding.
- communicate the requirements/lesson content clearly to pupils.
- show skill in gaining pupils' attention.
- show skill in voice and speech including good use of varying pitch and volume.
- convey interest and enthusiasm for the subject content.

1.2.7 contribute to the development of pupils' language and communication skills;
- demonstrate skill in asking and adapting questions.
- recognise the importance of literacy and oracy in pupils' learning.
- devise appropriate opportunities for pupils to develop their reading, writing and oracy skills.
- demonstrate awareness of the special needs of pupils for whom English is a second/third language.

1.2.8 demonstrate ability to select and use appropriate resources, including Information Technology;

- managing and organising settings and resources efficiently and sensitively — e.g. furniture, space, materials, audio visual aids, information technology.
- use computer software where appropriate and evaluate its contribution to teaching and learning.
- demonstrate a knowledge of health and safety in the learning environment.
- demonstrate awareness of support agencies which can offer resource advice for pupils with special educational needs.

1.3 CLASS MANAGEMENT
By the end of your course of initial training, newly qualified teachers should be able to:

1.3.1 decide when teaching the whole class, groups, pairs, or individuals is appropriate for particular learning purposes;
- see criteria 1.2.5.
- demonstrate awareness of the rest of the class when dealing with individuals/groups.

1.3.2 create and maintain a purposeful and orderly environment for the pupils;
- start and end sessions/lessons efficiently and effectively.
- demonstrate efficient planning and organisation of own time, including pacing and timing.
- make effective use of other support agencies in the classroom.

1.3.3 devise and use appropriate rewards and sanctions to maintain an effective learning environment;
- use praise and encouragement.
- use constructive feedback on achievement and behaviour.
- set appropriate learning targets and contracts.
- implement the whole school policy on pupil behaviour.

1.3.4 maintain pupils' interest and motivation;
- devise appropriate learning opportunities to maximise pupil achievement of objectives.
- show skill in gaining pupils' attention by imaginative presentation of the subject matter.
- show skill in voice and speech, good use of varying pitch and volume.
- use praise and encouragement through the use of profiling and records of achievement.

1.4 ASSESSMENT AND RECORDING OF PUPILS' PROGRESS

By the end of initial training, newly qualified teachers should be able to:

1.4.1 identify the current level of attainment of individual pupils using NCATs, statements of attainment and end of key stage statements where applicable;

- demonstrate an understanding of the place of the NC attainments in the wider achievements of the pupil, as recorded in the RoA.

1.4.2 judge how well each pupil performs against the standard expected of a pupil of that age;

- demonstrate an understanding of the cognitive development of pupils in the age range.
- use that understanding in the context of assessing pupil achievement.
- recognise the effects of teacher expectations and assessments on pupil achievement — see 1.6.7.
- understand the value and limitations of NCATs, SoAs and Standard Assessment Tasks in judging pupil performance.

1.4.3 assess and record systematically the progress of individual pupils;

- demonstrate a critical awareness of the wide range of assessment techniques available.
- understand and use formative and summative profile assessment and records of achievement.

1.4.4 use such assessment in their teaching;

- see 1.2.5.
- understand the varying purposes of assessment, including the differences between normative and criterion referencing.
- understand the value of formative assessment in maximising pupil achievement.
- use assessment and the knowledge this provides to devise appropriate learning opportunities.
- understand the value of self assessment and appraisal by others, including pupils.

1.4.5 demonstrate that they understand the importance of reporting to pupils on their progress and of marking their work regularly against agreed criteria;

- make those criteria explicit to pupils.

- involve pupils in regular formative assessment, target setting and action planning.
- demonstrate an awareness of the importance of reporting to parents on pupil progress — see 1.5.2.

1.5   CRITICAL SELF REFLECTION
Of subject knowledge and understanding: application, class management and assessment and recording of pupils' progress.

By the end of your course of initial training, newly qualified teachers should demonstrate the ability to:

1.5.1   analyse their own teaching performance;
- use a framework for an analysis of teaching and learning.
- use an appropriate balance between descriptive and analytical accounts of performance.
- use pupils' work/response to inform analysis.
- use information from analysis to inform future teaching.
- discuss intuition v technique as basis of performance.

1.5.2   appreciate the value of self assessment and assessment by others;
- accept and act on advice resulting from assessment.
- identify own strengths in performance.

1.5.3   identify their own professional development needs and the opportunities for meeting such needs;
- identify own professional development needs (match this with the views of others).
- demonstrate knowledge of opportunities and possible agencies/sources which could provide further professional development and enhance performance.
- continue this process of identification/response throughout professional career.
- appreciate the role that mentoring and appraisal can have in this process.

1.6   FURTHER PROFESSIONAL DEVELOPMENT
By the end of your initial training, newly qualified teachers should have acquired the necessary foundation to develop:

1.6.1   an understanding of the school as an institution and its place within the community;
- an understanding of the education system of England and Wales including the range of agencies available to support teaching and learning activities.

- an understanding of the organisation, management and general functions of schools.
- an understanding of the role of governing bodies, parents and the wider community in schools.
- an understanding of the importance of school — industry and school — community links programmes.
- an understanding of the role of the school in environmental issues.
- an understanding of the role of the school in the European and World Community.

1.6.2 a working knowledge of their pastoral, contractual, legal and administrative responsibilities as teachers;
- an understanding of the role of the form tutor.
- an understanding of the importance of personal and social education and active tutorial techniques for promoting PSE/ Health Education with pupils.
- an awareness of the importance of confidentiality and ethics.
- a knowledge of the 1988 Education Reform Act (ERA).
- a knowledge of the Parents' Charter and the Children Act.
- the knowledge of articles and instrument of government and power of the governing body.
- an understanding of the impact of LMS and delegated budgets and staffing powers on the role of the teacher.
- an understanding of Teachers Pay and Conditions of Employment.
- a clear understanding of their job description, key tasks and responsibilities.
- an understanding of their administrative responsibilities e.g. in recording and reporting achievement, attendance and truancy to parents.

1.6.3 an ability to develop effective working relationships with professional colleagues and parents, and to develop their communication skills;
- an ability to contribute effectively to professional discussions e.g. in staff meetings, in working groups and in professional development/appraisal interviews.
- skills in communicating with parents e.g. in reporting to parents, at parents' evenings, in community links programmes.
- an ability to develop listening, questioning, counselling, negotiating, constructive feedback, literacy and numeracy skills.

- an ability to work effectively in teams — to lead and be led where appropriate.
- an ability to contribute to the overall success of the school.

1.6.4   an awareness of individual differences, including social, psychological, developmental and cultural dimensions.

- an awareness of the issues and effects of racism and sexism in education.
- an understanding of the intellectual and physical development of pupils in the age range and the importance of that development on learning.
- an understanding of the effects of social and emotional disadvantage on learning.
- an understanding of the social and cultural backgrounds of pupils in the class/school.
- see also 1.2.4 and 1.2.5.

1.6.5   the ability to recognise diversity of talent including that of gifted pupils;

- a knowledge of the characteristics of higher level learning in subject(s).
- an awareness of the reasons for and symptoms of under achievement.
- the development of appropriate teaching and management strategies to incorporate individual differences and talents.

1.6.6   the ability to identify special educational needs or learning difficulties;

- the ability to identify Special Needs (in the context of the 1981 and 1988 Education Acts) may be made.
- the ability to develop appropriate teaching and management strategies, materials and resources to maximise learning.
- the ability to differentiate between those pupils whose needs can be met in the classroom and those requiring more specialised support.
- an understanding of school/LEA procedures relating to the statementing process.
- an understanding of the range of support agencies available.

1.6.7   a self critical approach to diagnosing and evaluating pupils learning, including a recognition of the effects on the learning of teachers' expectations.

- See 1.5 an understanding of the importance of critical self reflection in relation to subject knowledge, understanding, application, class management, assessment and recording of pupil progress.

- See 1.4.2 a recognition of the effects of teacher expectations and assessments on pupil learning.
- See 1.4.2 a recognition of the limitations of standard Assignment Tasks for diagnosing and evaluating pupils' learning and using formative assessments in a self-critical and sensitive manner.

1.6.8 a readiness to promote the moral and spiritual well-being of pupils.

- an ability to carry out the role of form tutor.
- a fulfilment of the pastoral role of the tutor (see 1.6.2) e.g. in relation to PSHE Programmes and links with the community.
- a recognition and respect for the differing spiritual beliefs of pupils, parents and colleagues.
- a fulfilment of the whole school policy on behaviour and codes of conduct.
- an ability to combat racism, sexism and other forms of prejudice in the behaviour, language and interactions of the school context.

1.6.9 a commitment to engage in on-going professional development throughout their career.

- a commitment to develop further their teaching and learning competences — including assessment.
- a commitment to develop further their professional competence — keeping up-to-date with developments in their subject areas.
- a commitment to develop further their wider professional competences — including management, co-ordination and liaison activities.
- a commitment to engage in professional debate and intellectual enquiry in relation to current educational issues e.g. special needs provision; GM status; appraisal, mentoring.

Appendix 2

2. **COMPETENCES EXPECTED OF NEWLY QUALIFIED TEACHERS (PRIMARY) — DFE (1993)**

2.1 Higher education institutions, schools and students should focus on the competences of teaching throughout the whole period of initial training. The progressive development of these competences should be monitored regularly during training. Their attainment at a level appropriate to newly qualified teachers should be the objective of every student taking a course of initial training.

Curriculum Content, Planning and Assessment
a) Whole Curriculum

2.2 Newly qualified teachers should be able to:

2.2.1 demonstrate understanding of the purposes, scope, structure and balance of the primary curriculum as a whole;

2.2.2 ensure continuity and progression within the work of their own class and with the classes to and from which their pupils transfer;

2.2.3 exploit in all their teaching opportunities to develop pupils' language, reading, numeracy and other skills.

b) Subject Knowledge and Application

2.3 Newly qualified teachers should be able to:

2.3.1 demonstrate relevant knowledge and understanding of the National Curriculum, including testing and assessment arrangements, in the core subjects and those other foundation subjects covered by their course;

2.3.2 plan lessons, teach, test and otherwise assess pupils in the core subjects of the National Curriculum and those other subjects of the primary curriculum covered in their course; newly qualified teachers may need guidance and support in some subjects.

c) Assessment and Recording of Pupils' Progress

2.4   Newly qualified teachers should be able to:

2.4.1   test, assess and record systematically the progress of individual pupils;

2.4.2   judge how well each pupil performs against appropriate criteria and standards by identifying individual pupils' levels of attainment, with reference to relevant National Curriculum requirements;

2.4.3   use such testing and assessment in their planning and teaching;

2.4.4   provide oral and written feedback to pupils on the processes and outcomes of their learning;

2.4.5   prepare and present reports on pupils' progress to parents.

Teaching Strategies
a) Pupils' Learning

2.5   Newly qualified teachers should be able to:

2.5.1   identify and respond appropriately to relevant individual differences between pupils;

2.5.2   show awareness of how pupils learn and of the various factors which affect the process;

2.5.3   demonstrate appropriate and demanding expectations of their pupils;

2.5.4   devise a variety and range of learning goals and tasks and monitor and assess them.

b) Teaching Strategies and Techniques

2.6   Newly qualified teachers should be able to:

2.6.1   establish clear expectations of pupil behaviour in the classroom and secure appropriate standards of discipline;

2.6.2   create and maintain a purposeful, orderly and supportive environment for their pupil's learning;

2.6.3   maintain pupils' interest and motivation;

2.6.4   present learning tasks and curriculum content in a clear and stimulating manner;

2.6.5   teach whole classes, groups and individuals, and determine the most appropriate learning goals and classroom contexts for using these and other teaching strategies;

2.6.6   use a range of teaching techniques, and judge when and how to deploy them;

2.6.7   employ varying forms of curriculum organisation, and monitor their effectiveness;

2.6.8   communicate clearly and effectively with pupils through questioning, instructing, explaining and feedback;

2.6.9   manage effectively and economically their own and their pupils' time;

2.6.10 select and use a range of resources for learning, including information technology;

2.6.11 train pupils in the individual and collaborative study skills necessary for effective learning.

Further Professional Development

2.7   Newly qualified teachers should have acquired in initial training the necessary foundation to develop;

2.7.1   a working knowledge of their contractual, legal, administrative and pastoral responsibilities as teachers;

2.7.2   effective working relationships with professional colleagues (including support staff) and parents;

2.7.3   the ability to recognise diversity of talent including that of gifted pupils;

2.7.4   the ability to identify and provide for special educational needs and specific learning difficulties;

2.7.5   the ability to evaluate pupils' learning, and recognise the effects on that learning of teachers' expectations and actions;

2.7.6   a readiness to promote the spiritual, moral, social and cultural development of pupils;

2.7.7   their professional knowledge, understanding and skill through further training and development;

2.7.8   vision, imagination and critical awareness in educating their pupils.

Appendix 3

School Management South — Management
Competences

An overview of the key purpose, key roles and units
of competence for school management

KEY PURPOSE

Create, maintain, review and develop the conditions which enable teachers and pupils to achieve effective learning

KEY ROLES AND FUNCTIONS

A Manage Policy	B Manage Learning	C Manage People	D Manage Resource

UNITS OF COMPETENCE

A1 Review, develop and present school aims, policies and objectives	B1 Review, develop and implement means for supporting pupils' learning	C1 Recruit and select teaching and non-teaching staff	D1 Secure effective resource allocation
A2 Develop supportive relationships with pupils, staff, parents, governors and the community	B2 Monitor and evaluate learning programmes	C2 Develop teams, individuals and self to enhance performance	D2 Monitor and control the use of resources
		C3 Plan, allocate and evaluate work carried out by teams, individuals and self	
		C4 Create, maintain and enhance effective working relationships	

School Management South 1992

Bibliography

Acton R, Kirkham G and Smith P (1992) *Mentoring – A Core Skills Pack* Crewe+ Alsager College of HE.

Arnold V and Davidson MJ (1990) 'Adopt a Mentor – the new way ahead for women managers?' in Davidson M J and Cooper C L *Shattering the Glass Ceiling: The Women Managers*, P.C.P.

Barret E (et al.) (1992) *Initial Teacher Education in England and Wales: A Topography*, ESRC Project (R000232810).

Bayliss S (1986) The Junior School Report, TES 18 April 1986.

Boon K P (1992) Evaluation of the Crewe+Alsager College of HE and Tameside MBC PGCE (Articled Teacher Scheme).

Booth M, Furlong J, Wilkin M (1990) *Partnership in Initial Teacher Training*, London, Cassell.

British Airways (1993) 'The Programme' (K Stevens).

Calderhead J and Lambert J (1992) *GTC England and Wales – The Induction of Newly Appointed Teachers*, NFER.

Cameron M (1993) Training for Preceptorship, Cheshire

CATE (1992) *The Accreditation of IIT under Circulars 9/92 (DFE) and 35/92 (Welsh Office) A Note of Guidance from CATE*, DFE.

Cheshire LEA (1993) *The First Year of Teaching*

Claxton G (1989) *Being a Teacher*, Cassell.

Crewe+Alsager College of HE (1990) Proposal for a Two Year PGCE Course for Articled Teachers.

Daresh J C and Playko M A (1992) *The Professional Development of School Administrators*, Allyn & Bacon.

Daresh J C and Playko M A (1993) *Leaders Helping Leaders*, Scholastic.

Davidson M and Cooper C (1992) *Women in Management*.

DES (1972) The James Committee *Teacher Education and Training*, London: HMSO.

DES (1987) *Quality in Schools: The Initial Training of Teachers*, London: HMSO.

DES (1989) LEATGS Draft Circular 1990–91.

DES (1990) *Developing School Management*, HMSO.

DES (1991) *Schools-based Initial Teacher Training in England and Wales*, London: HMSO.

DES (1991) E (School Teacher Appraisal) Regulations 4(2).

DFE (1991) Grants for Education Support and Training Draft Circular.

DFE (1992) Circular 9/92 *Initial Teacher Training (Secondary)*, DFE.

DFE (1992) Letter – School Teacher probation (22 July 1992) Teachers Branch.

DFE (1992) Administrative Memorandum 2/92 Induction of Newly Qualified Teachers (11 August 1992).

DFE (1992) Circular 9/92 Initial Teacher Training (Secondary Phase).

DFE (1993) *Schoolteachers' Pay and Conditions*, DFE.

DFE (1993) *Effective Management in Schools* – summary of NDC/CREATE project funded by DFE HMSO.

Drucker P (1989) *The New Realities*, Harper & Row.

Dunham J (1992) *Stress in Teaching*, (2nd edition), London: Routledge.

Earley P (1992) SMS Competences Report *A Guide to Evidence Collection and Assessment*, SMS, London: HMSO.

Employment Department (1993) *Investor in People*, Moorfoot, Sheffield.

Everard K B (1986) *Developing Management in Schools*, Oxford: Blackwell.

Garratt B (1987) *The Learning Organisation*, London: Fontana.

Green H, Holmes, G & Shaw, M (1991) Assessment and Mentoring for Headship, Oxford: EAC.

Handy C (1989) *The Age of Unreason*, London: Hutchison.

Haensly P A, and Edlind EP (1986) 'A search for ideal types in mentorship' *First International Conference on Mentoring*, Vancouver, B.C.

Hennig M and Jardin A (1979) *The Managerial Women*, London: Pan.

HMI/DES (1991) *School-based Initial Teacher Training in England and Wales*, London: HMSO.

Institute of Training and Development (1992) *Assessor and Verifier Awards* ITD, Marlow, Bucks.

Jacobi M (1991) *Mentoring and Undergraduate Academic Success*, A Literature Review, London: Education Research.

Joyce B and Showers B (1980) 'Improving in-service training', Educational Leadership, **37**(s).

Karpf A (1993) 'Convincing a worker that she's as good as her word', *The Guardian* 21.6.93.

Katz D and Kahn Rl (1978) *The Social Psychology of Organizations* (2nd edition) New York, Wiley.

Khalifa Al (1989) 'Management by halves: women teachers and school management' in De Lyon H and Widdowson Migniuolo (eds) *Women Teachers: Issues and Experiences*, OUP.

Khalifa Al (1993) *Equal Opportunities and Appraisal* An INSET session at Liverpool University 1993.

King C (eds) with Anderson M, Robinson A and West-Burnham J (1993) *Through the Glass Ceiling: Effective Management Development for Women*, Hodder and Stoughton.

Kyriacou (1987) 'Teacher stress and burn out: an international review' in *Human Resource Management*, Riches C and Morgan C, OUP.

Kram K E (1985) *Mentoring at Work; Developmental Relationships in Organizational Life*, Scott, Foresman.

Langtree Conference and Training Centre (1993) 'What Evidence does a School Produce' Standish Community High School.

The Management Charter Initiative (1992) *The School Management Handbook*, London: Kogan Page.

Margerison C (1991) *Making Management Development Work*, McGraw-Hill.

Merriam S (1983) 'Mentors and proteges: a critical review of the literature' *Adult Education Quarterly*, **33**:161–173.

Mortimer P (1988) *School Matters: The Junior Years*, Open Books.

NAHT (1993) (i) *The role of the mentor in school-based initial teacher training.* NAHT pamphlet. (ii) *School-based initial teacher training.* NAHT pamphlet.

NASUWT (1993) *Teacher Induction Policy Statement.*

Nias, J, Southwork, G and Yeomans, R (1989) *Staff Relationships in the Primary School*, A study of organizational cultures, London: Cassell.

OFSTED (1992) *Handbook for the Inspection of Schools*, OHMCI.

OFSTED (1993) *The New Teacher in School – A Survey by HMI in England and Wales.*

Oliver J (1993) *Headstart*, NEAC.

Pay Review Board (1993) *Report 1993*, London: HMSO.

Pomeroy R (1993) *Survey of current and anticipated Mentor Training Programmes*, University of Wolverhampton.

Quinlan K (1991) *Cheshire Education Management Programme*, Cheshire Education Services.

Revans R (1980) *Action Learning*, Blond and Briggs.

Rutter M (1979) *Fifteen Thousand Hours* Open Books.

Salford Compact (1993) *First and Second National Conferences*, In association with E D and Whitbread plc.

School Management South (1992) *The School Management Competences Project*, Final report. London: HMSO.

School Management Task Force (1990) Report. DES.

School Teachers' Review Body (1993) Second Report, London: HMSO.

Schon D (1983) *The Reflective Practitioner*, London: Random House.

Schon D (1987) *Educating the Reflective Practitioner*, London: Jossey Bass.

Schon D, Sergiovanni T, and Carbally J (1994) 'Leadership as reflection in action' in *Leadership and Organisational Culture*, University of Illinois Press.

Segerman-Peck L M (1991) *Networking and Mentoring: A Women's Guide*, London: Piatkus.

Shapiro E C, Haseltine F, and Rowe M (1978) 'Moving up: role models, mentors and the patron system' Sloan Management Review, **19**:51–58.

Shea G F (1992) *Mentoring*, London: Kogan Page.

Shepherd, G (1993) 'Targets we must hit', *Times Educational Supplement* 2 April 1993 p.16.

Shipman M (1990) *In Search of Learning*, Oxford: Blackwell.

Smith P (1992) *A Guide to mentoring in the Secondary School – a competency-based approach*, Manchester Metropolitan University.

Smith P and Wall M (1993) NQT/Mentor Training Session – Tameside 8 July 1993.

Tameside MBC and Faculty of Crewe+Alsager (1993) Professional Development Profile for Newly Qualified Teachers.

Torrington D and Weightman J (1989) *The Reality of School Management*, Oxford: Blackwell.

Trethowan P (1991) *Managing with Appraisal*, P.C.P.

United Kingdom Central Council for Nursing, Midwifery and Health Visiting (1993) Registrars letter 4 January 1993, Annex one.

Wall M (1990) Articled Teacher Scheme, Report to the Education Services Committee.

Weindling D and Earley P (1987) *Secondary Headships, The First Years*, Windsor NFER – Nelson.

West-Burnham J (1993) *The Appraisal Training Resource Manual*, Harlow: Longman.

Wilkin, M (1992) *Area Groups for ITT* – a discussion paper.

Wood S (1988) *Continuous Development*, IPM.